£29-95,

/

STRESS, SELF-CONCEPT, and VIOLENCE

Stress in Modern Society: No. 11

Other Titles in This Series:
No. 1. James H. Humphrey, ed. *Stress in Childhood,* 1984.
No. 2. James H. Humphrey. *Profiles in Stress,* 1986.
No. 3. Joy N. Humphrey and James H. Humphrey. *Coping with Stress in Teaching,* 1986.
No. 4. George S. Everly, Jr. and Stephen A. Sobelman. *Assessment of the Human Stress Response,* 1987.
No. 6. Jerrold S. Greenberg. *Stress and Sexuality.* 1987.
No. 8. John Sullivan and Joyce Cameron Foster. *Stress and Pregnancy.* 1989.
No. 10. A. J. W. Taylor. *Disasters and Disaster Stress.* 1989.
No. 12. Amarjit S. Sethi. *Meditation As an Intervention in Stress Reactivity.* 1989.
No. 13. Judity L. Hanna. *Dance and Stress: A Holistic Approach to Dealing with Stress.* 1988.
No. 15. Lilian Rosenbaum. *Biofeedback Frontiers: Self-Regulation of Stress Reactivity.* 1989.
No. 16. M. Lawrence Furst and Donald R. Morse. *The Woman's World.* 198 .
No. 17. Donald R. Morse and Robert L. Pollack. *Nutrition, Stress, and Aging: An Holistic Approach.* 1988.
No. 18. James H. Humphrey. *Children and Stress: Theoretical Perspectives and Recent Research.* 1988.
No. 19. Donald R. Morse and Robert L. Pollack. *The Stress-Free, Anti-Aging Diet.* 1989.

Stress in Modern Society
Number 11

Stress, Self-Concept, and Violence

John A. Corson, Ph.D.
Dartmouth Medical School
and
Dartmouth College in New Hampshire
Veterans Administration in Vermont

AMS PRESS, INC.
New York

Library of Congress Cataloging-in-Publications Data

Corson, John A.
    Stress, self-concept, and violence / John A. Corson.
        p.   cm.
    Bibliography: p.
    Includes index.
    ISBN 0-404-63263-7
    1. Stress (Psychology) 2. Self-perception. 3. Violence-
    Psychological aspects. I. Title.
    RC455.4.S87C67   1989
    616.85'82--dc19   86-82026

All AMS books are printed on acid-free paper that meets the
guidelines for performance and durability of the Committee
on Production Guidelines for Book Longevity of the
Council on Library Resources.

AMS PRESS
56 East 13th Street
New York, N.Y. 10003, U.S.A.

Manufactured in the United States of America

CONTENTS

Acknowledgments   xi

Introduction   xiii

    Self-Concept and Stress
    Positive Expectancies and Failure Signals
    Individual Differences
    Learning and Memory, Mathematics and Neurophysiology
    Nomothetic Research
    Biological Variables
    Stress and Individual Differences
    Overview

PART ONE: Theory and Strategy

Chapter One - An Ideographic Approach to Theory   **1**

    Systems Theory and Modeling Applied to Individuals
    A Blueprint
    Minimodels
    Definitions and Postulates
        Stress
        Self-Concept

Chapter Two - A Shifty Theory of Personality   **11**

Shifty Definition
Shifting Biases
Violent Clients as Examples for Theorizing
Self-Concept: Stable Constructs
    The Compelling Situation
    The Possible Self
    The Working Self
    The Essential Audience
    The Personal Scientist/Theorist
Self Concept: Shifting Variables
    The Binary Switch
    The Quality of Internal Dialogue
Summary

**Chapter Three - Biological Variables
in Personality**   **25**

The Sympathetic Nervous System:
    An Emotional Fire in the Boiler
Central Motive State
Central Motive State, Working Self, Personal Theorist
    and Point of View
Summary

PART TWO: Lessons from the Family

**Chapter Four - Families as Mutual
Control Systems**   **37**

Parental Attention
Mutual Control Systems
Reinforcement and Learning
The Development of Self-Concept
Summary

Chapter Five - The Family Optimization Program   **55**

    Application with Normal Families
    The Contract
    Systematic Parental Attention
    Physical Punishment
    Some Data
    Application With Troubled Families
    A Boy With Problems
    Abusive Parents
    Summary
    Advantages

Chapter Six - Troubled Families with Preverbal Children   **71**

    The Time - Out Procedure
    Mr. D.
    Advantages

Chapter Seven - Troubled Adults   **83**

    Mismanaged Parental Attention
    Incentive Stimuli Inverted
    Tracing Back

PART THREE: Technique

Chapter Eight - Assessment Approaches   **91**

    Some Options
    The ABC Chart

Chapter Nine - The Flow Diagram   **97**

    Procedure
    Applications
    Other Uses
    Client as Coinvestigator
    Evaluation Issues

Chapter Ten - Biofeedback   **107**

    General Method
    An Application With Pain and Spasms
    Other Applications
    Evaluation
    Practice Issues
    Other Problems
    A Technique for Profiling

PART FOUR: Violent Adults

Chapter Eleven - A Selective Literature Review   **117**

    Neurological Correlates
    Early Environment
    Hyperarousal and the Binary Switch
    Level - setting Functions of the ANS
    Self-Concept
       Looking for Trouble
    Secondary Gains
    Critics, Heroes, and Monsters
    Therapeutic Possibilities
    A New Self-Concept
    Seizures
    Recommended Reading

Chapter Twelve - Population, Treatment Method, and Results   **133**

    Sample
    Assessment and Treatment Methods
    Phase I
    Phase II
    Phase III
    Results and Discussion
        Record Keeping
        Follow–up
        Physiological Data
    Possible Explanations

Chapter Thirteen - Case Histories and Treatment Details   **161**

    Mr. A
    Mr. B
    Mr. C
    Mr. D
    Treatment Adaptations
    Mr. G
    Mr. K
    Ms. E

Chapter Fourteen - Theoretical Perspectives and Practical Advice   **215**

    Self-Concept and Violent Behavior
    Response to the Violent Person
    When Someone Threatens Others
    When Someone Threatens You

Conclusion 223

Assessment and Treatment
Biofeedback
Violent Behavior
Personality and Society

References 229
Index 239

Acknowledgements

First, I thank my wife and children for their patience and support throughout this project.

This book summarizes several aspects of my work over the last 25 years. The work was made possible by the support and help I have received from many friends and colleagues, and by the participation of hundreds of clients. I am grateful to the parent of a Dartmouth graduate who anonymously donated a fund to support research on stress. This has made an important difference in the type and amount of work I have been able to do.

I am deeply indebted to Carolyn Mercer-McFadden, Ph.D., and Dana Grossman for editing and good-natured support and guidance. I thank Peg Pearson, Sandra Lukash and Pam Burnett for typing and retyping (and retyping again). We all thank the inventors of the word processor. I thank David Kingston for making all the word processors talk to each other and for formatting this book.

Many colleagues worked directly with me on the development and testing of procedures for assessment and treatment of violent adults. Three who were particularly involved in the early phases are Bruce Vogel, Mary Schneider and Robin Hill. I am indebted to many other colleagues who put these procedures to work with many troubled and troublesome clients.

I have shared parts of this book with some of my clients. Each of the four men described in Chapter 13 has read the section pertaining to him. Each is the co-author of the section pertaining to him. I asked my clients to help me with the demographic features in order to ensure the degree of anonymity they would be comfortable with. They wanted only minimal changes if any — and I have added a few other changes. I also asked them to add, subtract or edit anything from details to interpretations. They made no subtractions and few additions.

One of these men wrote an eloquent objection to the use of the word "client." He preferred the word "patient" or "person." "Client" reminded him of a relationship based on a commercial transaction, and seemed to transform the person or patient into an object. I thought for a long time about this. In fact I had initially used the word "patient." Finally I decided to go ahead with the word client, with the realization that there are some people who will be upset by any word I use here.

I realize also that everyone will be deeply upset by some of the things included in this book. The people who have been my clients have been tormented, and they have tormented others. Many have killed other people. Most who were killed were killed in wartime combat or paracombat situations, but some were killed in peacetime. The misery, fear and unfairness of their lives and many of the lives they have touched make this whole project a sad burden for me and for my clients. I am thankful that they have had the energy, ability and motivation to join me in this project. I hope the ideas and methods presented here will in the future help to prevent and deal with violent behavior.

Introduction

I will begin this book with some personal history to show you how I have come to be interested in the relationship between self-concept and stressful experiences. (I will explain my interest in violence later.)

Self-Concept and Stress

When I was three, my father died. My mother was distraught. She was also attempting to deal with my younger brother who was then only a few months old. My world came apart. I had been limping along with the beginnings of a self-concept, developed in a supportive and admiring family system. Suddenly I confronted one of the most stressful experiences in life.

Positive Expectancies
and Failure Signals

Soon I became interested in the demerit system that was used in my grade school. I brought it home to my aunt, who was struggling to help me grow up. She and I worked out our own version of this system. Our system implied an expectation of good behavior, listed unacceptable behaviors as well as the consequences for them, and ensured 30-60 minutes of individual adult attention each day. It worked for us. The system persists today. First, with only minor alterations, it serves as a format for optimizing management of parental attention to children (see Chapter 5), and second, with more extensive alterations, it is a method for managing some aspects of the operation of hospital wards.

Individual Differences

An important watershed occurred when I was in high school. My homeroom teacher asked us all to write a page about what we wanted to do with our lives. Instead of regurgitating what had been my stock answer, wanting to be a surgeon like my father, I gave it a few seconds of thought and realized that I wanted to study individual differences. I was fascinated by the differences among people. I assumed that many differences among people had been caused by differences in experience and learning, which would lead to the formation of memories, which, in turn, would create the behavioral dispositions that we see as individual differences. In that one page, I boiled it all down to finding out more about the processes of learning and memory.

In college my reading of Adler convinced me that self-concept is a central issue in psychology and is a key to understanding individual differences. My undergraduate research in psychology was a cumbersome attempt to examine the role of self-concept in determining how different individuals cope with failure signals.

Learning and Memory,
Mathematics and Neuropsychology

Shortly after completing this experiment, I decided to go to graduate school to see what Adlerian psychology had to offer in the study of individual differences. Heinz Ansbacher, an expert on Adler, was at the University of Vermont, and so I applied there. By a stroke of luck the only person there who was able to provide funds to support a graduate student was Norman J. Slamecka, who was studying the learning process. Thus I was also able to pursue my high school plans: to examine individual differences by way of studying the process of learning and memory. While working in Norm Slamecka's lab, I came up with some odd ideas about the early stages of memory formation, in particular some ideas about what happens in serial learning when one attempts and fails to retrieve a specific item of information. I developed a simple neurological model and a mathematical version that was testable. Eventually I found that the model only worked for serial learning and not for paired-associate learning. However, I was hooked on modeling.

At around the time I was finishing my master's thesis, I came across Donald Hebb's presidential address to the American Psychological Association (1960), which was reprinted in the American Psychologist under the title " The American Revolution." In this magnificent piece, Hebb described his attempts as a psychologist to understand neurological ideas and to make them work as part of a model or theory that would cast light on human behavior. Again I was hooked. I found out about his book *Organization of Behavior* (1949) and read it from cover to cover. At about that time I also read a statistics text by George Ferguson(1959) and a book on motivation by Dalbir Bindra(1959). A very important moment came when I realized that Hebb, Ferguson, and Bindra were all at McGill University. I applied for admission to the graduate psychology program at McGill and was eventually accepted as one of Hebb's students.

Nomothetic Research

Both Hebb and Slamecka tried to shift my attention away from individual differences, and to guide me into a more careful consideration of the nomothetic quest, the search for possible generalizations. I complied with their urging and focused in my doctoral thesis on the acquisition and retention of discrimination habits in rats. Some of the data led me back circuitously to consider individual differences. Specifically, I had gathered some data suggesting that acquisition of a memory when the subject is in a particular mood biases the probability of later retrieval, making it easier to retrieve that memory when the mood, or emotional state, that pertained during learning is reinstated at the time of the attempt to retrieve the memory. These ideas led me into a post-doctoral fellowship with the eminent physiologist-physician R.A. Cleghorn.

Biological Variables

One result of my association with Cleghorn was the exposure to his research, clinical interests and experience. One paper in particular had a profound influence. This was an observation by Cleghorn and Pattee (1954) of opposite emotional and cognitive effects of steroid injections on two adult subjects: one person became manic and another person became deeply depressed. This study helped to focus and provide a possible explanation for some of the odd findings I had obtained with my laboratory animals.

Stress and Individual Differences

During this period, with Selye only a few hundred yards away, I became more deeply interested in reading and thinking about individual differences in response to stress. I read numerous theoretical articles and reviews. Eventually I saw that although most of this literature started out by generating complex and nomothetic (group) hypotheses, the conclusion was often along the lines of, "Gee whiz, look how complex and multivariate this relationship is...Perhaps if variables A through Z are just so, then the following nomothetic law will apply X percent of the time."

At this point I decided to refocus my interests on individual differences. And that is what this book is all about.

Overview

This introduction has set the stage for a multilevel, systems theory of human behavior and has alluded to some related issues and methods.

Part One of this book presents this theory as it pertains to stress, self-concept, and personality. Chapter 1 briefly introduces an individualistic strategy for thinking about stress and self-concept. Chapter 2 integrates this system into a "shifty" theory of personality. Chapter 3 continues the consideration of the personality theory, but focuses on biological variables.

Part Two contains four chapters about families, personality development, and behavioral problems. Chapter 4 considers developmental influences on personality. Chapter 5 presents a program for optimizing these developmental influences and presents data on use of this system with normal families and with troubled families. Chapter 6 describes a program, and some results, for working with families who have preverbal children. Chapter 7 focuses again on the development of the individual personality and specifically considers what happens "when things go wrong."

Part three contains three chapters dealing with technique. Chapter 8 describes approaches to assessment of stress, stressors, and personality. Chapter 9 presents a format – the flow diagram – for organizing thoughts and data on stressors and the self-concept and for planning treatment of troubled adults. Chapter 10 reviews the present status of biofeedback, and briefly details a biofeedback technique that my colleagues and I have used in the assessment and treatment of violent adults.

Introduction

Part four consists of four chapters about violent behavior and my work with violent adults. Chapter 11 is a selective review of literature on violent adults. Chapters 12 and 13 present theory, methods, data and case histories of patients referred for violent behavior. Chapter 14 provides some reflections on the violent personality and some practical observations and suggestions.

The conclusion reviews key points from the earlier chapters and stresses the importance of continuing attention to the evolving reciprocal relationship between stressors and self-concept.

Part One

Theory and Strategy

1 : An Ideographic Approach to Theory

My focus now – and the focus of this book – can be characterized as follows: "Here is a stressed individual, or an individual who is having trouble coping with some or all sorts of stress. What can we do to understand and to help this person improve his or her quality of life?"

It is clear that, even with this focus, we still have to deal with a multitude of variables. However, we have a theory that seems to help. This theory treats self-concept as the superordinate variable; it spells out developmental relationships among parental attention, sense of self, and the selection of incentive stimuli; and it traces these relationships to their manifestations in the behavior of the adult.

With my colleagues, I have also developed a few strategies and procedures that appear to help. This book describes the theory, the strategies, some data, and some remaining problems and possibilities. Much of the context for this book is provided by case histories of specific people in extremely stressful situations. The focal point in attempting to understand these people is their sense of self or self-concept.

Systems Theory and Modeling Applied to Individuals

Until recently, most systems theorizing and modeling attempts in psychology were conducted in the nomothetic (group) arena. However, for the time being, it seems more fruitful to work at the ideographic (individual) level and to use systems thinking and modeling to deal with individuals and with the specific activities of specific individuals. My first formal introduction to systems thinking and modeling was in the mid-sixties in a course offered to graduate students and faculty members at McGill University by John Milsum, a pioneer in systems thinking, modeling, and biomedical engineering. Much of the course focused on modeling systems of regional temperature regulation in living organisms. However, it was clear that these strategies could be put to work in the analysis of other systems.

A Blueprint

The term "biopsychosocial" summarizes a systems concept (e.g., see Engel, 1980) that has been alluded to for generations. The notion has been around for a long time: everything that a human being experiences and does is influenced by and influences everything else that he or she experiences and does.

A few years ago a summer symposium at Dartmouth College was considering the topic of reciprocal determinism among biological, psychological, and social variables in alcoholism. We were attempting to develop models of alcoholism using strategies of systems dynamics. I was in a minority who pushed for modeling an individual alcoholic rather than modeling all alcoholics at once, or to model alcoholism. As one result of this symposium, a student produced a master's thesis that did indeed focus on modeling the biological, psychological, and social variables in the life of a single alcoholic. This model dealt with the phenomenon of multiple and reciprocal influences bearing on a single outcome; the model represented a hierarchical system with sense of self, or self-concept, as a superordinate variable.

In the last several years, my colleagues and I have applied such modeling strategies to individual clients with other problems, most frequently to clients referred to us for outbursts of violent behavior.

As will be spelled out in later chapters, we have learned that large and formal models are not as useful in assessing and treating an individual's problems as are a variety of mini-models regarding specific behaviors in specific situations. In fact, the utility of these mini-models, or throw-away models, is much greater than we had originally anticipated.

Mini-Models

My colleagues and I have found that our general theory and modeling strategy can quite easily be explained to most clients. We have also found that many clients are able to grasp the ideas of reciprocal determination and biopsychosocial modeling best if we select a single episode in their lives and work out a tentative mini-model around this episode. The procedure will be detailed later, but a brief example will help at this point. With numerous clients, we have been able to use physiological monitoring procedures, television feedback of facial expression and verbal behavior, and role-playing, along with various strategies for assessing the interaction of self-satisfaction with specific life situations, to create a multilevel model of a specific episode from real life. Figure 1.1 shows the set-up and equipment for using all aspects of this strategy. Table 1.1 shows the total format for gathering the data and ideas in preparation for using the strategy. (We often use only a part of this format, and as will soon be seen, we also use many other ways of gathering data and developing ideas.)

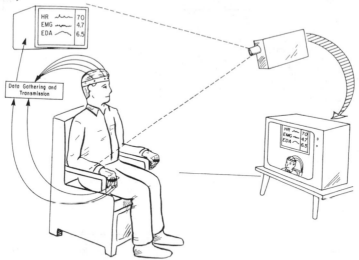

Figure 1.1. *Physiological monitoring system combined with TV system to provide feedback to the client of both biological and behavioral variables. This is used both for simultaneous feedback (e.g., during a role-playing situation) and for later playback.*

Table 1.1

Format for Gathering Information About a Behavioral Episode

PERSONAL SCIENCE–FORMAT FOR DEVELOPING A MULTILEVEL **ABC** DIAGRAM:

Use this format to describe the most recent (or most memorable) occurrence of your problem and fill in as many of the spaces as you can.

ANTECEDENTS: Ask yourself what was going on in yourself and your environment just before the problem occurred;

BEHAVIORS: Ask yourself what behavior did you show and what was going on in yourself and environment during the behavioral episode;

CONSEQUENCES: Ask youself what happened after the behavioral episode ended.

		ANTECEDENTS	BEHAVIORS	CONSEQUENCES
THINGS OTHER PEOPLE	DO			
	SAY			
OTHER ENVIRONMENTAL EVENTS				
MY OVERT BEHAVIOR				
MY COVERT BEHAVIOR THOUGHTS				
MOODS, EMOTIONS & FEELINGS				
LABELS I USE FOR MYSELF				
THE LEVEL OF MY SELF ESTEEM	HIGH			
	MEDIUM			
	LOW			
THE LEVEL OF MY EXCITEMENT	HIGH			
	MEDIUM			
	LOW			

Recently, we were able to use this format with a violent client to help him develop insight into the following processes:

(1) A cumulative biological priming influences his behavioral dispositions in certain social situations.

(2) His own stimulus value (his face and posture) is likely to have a "feed forward" effect in a social situation. Specifically, before he says anything, or interacts with anyone in a social situation, he influences other people by his menacing facial expression and his threatening posture. Thus, the first response that anyone makes to him is already influenced by the other person's responses to a certain perceived level of threat resulting from his presence and presentation.

(3) The realization of his stimulus value (an interpretation of his facial expression and posture) led this client to a description of certain expectancies, about people trying to humiliate him, and response dispositions, about his unwillingness to permit this to happen.

This simple reenactment of a real-life experience led to a mini-biopsychosocial model that depicted a complex, multifaceted system of influences, that facilitated insight by the client, and that brought about eventual dramatic improvement in his behavior.

Definitions and Postulates

Stress

Defining stress has long been considered problematic[1]. Definitions are often relative, and frequently tautological. Here, where I consider stress from an individual point of view in association with self-concept, the relativism and even the inherent tautology become functional rather than problematic.

Selye, in the late 1930's, proposed a distinction between the cause of bodily disturbance and its effect. He referred to the external cause, or the stimulus, as a stressor, and to the state of

---

[1] Everly and Sobelman (1987) have recently addressed the issues of definition and assessment of stress.

bodily disequilibrium, or the response, as stress. This bare-bones definition has been widely accepted, but it does not address several important issues – for example, the extent to which stress responses are nonspecific and the extent to which stress is good or bad.

Selye (1974,1976) summarized some of his views in the following way:

(1)   Stress is nonspecific, although each stressor has both specific effects (sweating during heat) and nonspecific effects (the adrenal enlargement, the thymus involution, and the development of ulcers that may occur if a stress continues for a long enough period of time).

(2)   A stressor is whatever produces these nonspecific effects (admittedly a circular definition).

(3)   Psychological events can produce the same stress responses as physical stressors.

(4)   Some stressors produce good stress (Selye (1978) called this "eustress", a mixture of the words euphoria and stress). Other stressors produce bad stress (this he called "distress").

(5)   Stress is always a matter of degree.

(6)   Stress in human beings can be moderated by various treatment techniques.

In current usage, we do not consistently distinguish between eustress and distress. In fact, we typically use the word stress to denote both the stimulus and its effects, including internal (psychological, emotional, and physiological) and behavioral responses.

As pointed out by Selye, the stressor, or stimulus, can come from many sources: Bright lights, loud noises, social interactions, anticipation of an exam, a disturbing thought, a sore throat – the list is endless. Clearly, the stimulus can be internal or external to the individual experiencing stress.

The nature of the stress response also varies widely. Stress responses may include changes in respiration, changes in perspiration, diarrhea, disturbing thoughts, dry mouth, crying, swearing, fatigue – again the list is endless.

As noted in the 1967 work of Holms and Rahe, even a pleasant stimulus such as getting married or giving birth to a child, can produce a wide variety of responses, reflecting both pleasure and displeasure. Such a complex state of affairs suggests that we might be wise to stop using the word stress. But I will continue to use the word, identifying the stimulus and its effects as specifically as possible, and I will place the concept of stress within an individual framework and a systems theory.

Self-Concept

To make any sense of the idea of multiple causality interacting with individual differences, we need a multilevel systems theory. I am convinced that the superordinate role in this theory must be played by the individual's self-concept.

Just as stressor and stress are redefined for each individual and for each new situation that the person interacts with, self-concept is relative. Self-concept changes with each instance in which an individual interacts with a particular stressor and experiences a stress response.

Now you may want to throw up your hands in despair! But I urge you to stay with me for a while. I have developed some strategies, specific formats, mnemonic devices, and simple routines which help me and will help you to think quickly and flexibly about these shifting complexities. I expect that it will be quite easy for you to follow the strategies and evaluate the ideas. The reasons for this approach are compelling.

Two of the most compelling reasons are that the important clinical data are variable, and that within nonclinical, or "normal", samples intraindividual variations are significant. I will argue these points from experience.

Long ago, I realized that these variables seen clinically were in constant flux. This realization led me to develop a very simple method (described in detail later) to keep track of the relationships between different situations and different levels of self-satisfaction, or status of self-concept. At each session I use a format that quickly determines the client's highest and lowest levels of self-satisfaction in the preceeding 24 hours, and in what situations the client experienced these high and low levels. The results further convinced me that intraindividual variations – even within a day – are so wide that any of the existing theories of personality would simply not suffice. Furthermore, any existing assessment procedure – whether it be a complicated personality test or a psychophysiological profile – taken at any specific time would not do a good job of predicting the relationships between situations and behavior patterns for any particular client. Rather, the predictive ability increased as I saw the client in session after session and gathered data about relationships concerning specific interactions between situations and behavior. As the years went by, and as I met with and consulted about more and more clients, I became convinced that this highly individualized approach to the person and the situation is essential. I also saw that such an approach was a prerequisite for eventually developing some rules about the organization of behavior and some general concepts regarding individual differences.

The second experience which convinced me of the need for this approach to stress, self-concept, and situations was a study I conducted in collaboration with 22 Dartmouth College students in the fall of 1978. These students were registered in my course on individual differences and served as both co-experimenters and subjects. For 14 consecutive days during the term, they monitored daily their highest and their lowest levels of self-satisfaction, or self-concept, on 21 bipolar continua, and they made notes regarding the situations that corresponded with the three highest and the three lowest ratings of each of the 14 days. They analyzed and reported on their own patterns of behavior in a wide variety of situations and carefully noted how the interactions between themselves and the situations were reflected in – and, in varying degrees, driven by – the status of their own self-concept at the time of experiencing each particular situation. The students also completed a variety of tests[2]: Rotter's locus-of-control scale; Rathus's assertiveness scale; Eysenck's introvert-extrovert scale, Jenkins's activity scale; the Adjective Check List; the Tennessee Self-Concept Scale; a "personal constructs" test modified from work done by Kelly (1955); and a physiological stress profile that monitored biological variables (skin conductance and temperature) during a period of relaxation, a period of stress, and a final period of relaxation (see Chapter 10). The students also worked on the development and use of a device that monitored the incentive quality of a variety of stimulus situations and the pattern of behavior related to those situations.

This project resulted in a massive and multifaceted data base. Fortunately the class consisted of some of the most able students I have ever met. At the end of the course we developed a collective synthesis and overview. The fundamental conclusion was that

---

[2] References to all published tests mentioned in the book are provided in the three following sources: Buros (1974), Newmark (1985), Sweetland and Keyser (1983).

while some general consistencies did appear, the intraindividual variability in this sample of healthy and intelligent young people was truly remarkable. No existing personality theory can encompass these variations adequately (although some have tried, for example, Epstein (1980) and Mischel (1976)).

Another observation, made by almost every student, is reflected in the following feedback. "Professor Corson, thanks for what turned out to be a very worthwhile experience. The course opened my eyes to a lot of issues I would never have considered otherwise, and working on the incentive survey gave me more satisfaction than any other project." In a later telephone conversation, the student told me that his experience with the course had led him to think of himself and his likes and dislikes in a totally new way and to dramatically alter his career plans.

Such feedback suggests that the essence of a stable sense of self, and stabilities in likes and dislikes regarding situations, can indeed be distilled by a well-informed observer from a mass of data gathered over a long enough time. Over the years, this approach has enabled me to gather the data that now provide the basis of what I like to call a "shifty theory of personality."

2 : A Shifty Theory of Personality

Human behavior is remarkably complex and variable. A good theory of personality (particularly one that specifies person-situation relationships in proper detail) can prevent the scientist or clinician from being overwhelmed by human diversity and by the intraindividual differences as a particular subject or client passes through time and through various life situations.

Shifty Definition

When I am asked about personality by psychology students, or when I hear them attempting to describe someone's personality, I ask them to consider the definition of personality. "Tell me what behavior makes you say this person has personality X, and then tell me what situation is most likely to cause that person to show this X-type behavior." And that's it! *Personality is a description of specific behavior patterns in specific situations.* To go any further toward understanding personality, we must focus on a single person. We must perform a microanalysis of the various domains or aspects of the behavior pattern and its relationships to the particular situation. The theory by definition is only good for one person. But some variable aspects of all behavior-situation interactions are as follows:

(1) Environmental events,
(2) The subject's overt behavior as time passes and as the behavior is modified by environmental events,
(3) The subject's covert behavior, including cognitive and emotional states,

(4)   The subject's changes in arousal level,
(5)   The subject's changes in self-concept and self-satisfaction.

This list is not exhaustive, but it gives you an idea about the range of ever-changing variables involved in personality. The list also sets the stage for our further elaboration of what I call "a shifty[1] theory of personality."

Shifting Biases

Theorizing about personality has always been a shifty proposition. Allport in 1937 surveyed the literature on theories and definitions of personality and – even those five decades ago – came up with a vast array of ideas about personality.

He found more than 40 different definitions of personality in the literature. One of the problems in the field, reflected by Allport's observations, is the remarkable range of values and preferred points of view, or biases, among those who have attempted to scientifically observe and define personality. The differences among the theorists in their biases about personality are related to differences in their samples of subjects or clients. Freud, for example, was exposed to many troubled people. Cattell, on the other hand, was an experimental psychologist who spent more time studying relatively normal subjects. Thus Freud's theory and definitions include different aspects from Cattell's.

As should by now be clear, my own values and biases about personality theory have evolved from my clinical experience. In that regard, I have had the good fortune of working with a famous gastroenterologist, Dr. Thomas Almy. While Almy would not call himself a personality theorist, I have learned many things from him about personality theory. Almy carries an implicit personality theory and strategy into each new clinical interaction. He developed, years ago, the strategy of using a "life chart." (Almy & Corson, 1987). This life chart relates the events in a person's life to various gastrointestinal and other medical symptoms. The life chart allowed Almy to simplify and to relate to each other various

---

[1] The word *shifty* – shift in adjectival form – is defined by Webster's as 1: resourceful, 2a: tricky; b: elusive. I use the word *shifty* to connote how constantly *resourceful* we must be in dealing with the multitude of *tricky* and *elusive* variables that constitute personality.

behavior patterns, symptoms and experiential events so that the complex symphony of life of a person in various situations would become more clear. Almy's life chart strategy also affirmed my bias toward microanalysis, minimodels, and an individualistic approach.

Violent Clients as Examples for Theorizing

My approach in this theory-development exercise will draw heavily from a fairly narrow data base on a relatively small sample of especially troubled people. I have many reasons for selecting this group of people, and they will all become obvious as we go along.

One very good reason for choosing this group is that people who have violent outbursts scare us. Specifically they scare me. I find that the activity of developing a theory not only reduces the complexities, but theorizing also reduces my fear, as it increases my sense of understanding and control over the client's behavior.

Another important reason for choosing violent clients is that I have had extensive experience with this group. My sample consists of people who have been referred for assessment and treatment of their problems with violent outbursts over the last 20 years. I have known, or have had complete access to data concerning, over 300 people with these problems. Between 1974 and 1984, at the White River Junction VA, 115 people were referred to the Psychology Section for these problems (out of about 1,100 in all referred to the Psychology Section). Between 1964 and 1974, while I was at McGill, approximately 3,000 people were referred to our clinical group, and about 10 percent of these people were referred for violent outbursts.

Finally, in addition to the personal importance of violent clients to all of us, and the availability to me of their data, my reasons for choosing as examples the clients prone to violent behavior are conceptually pragmatic:

(1) The behavior is relatively dramatic and salient.
(2) The behavior is easy to describe and to operationalize.
(3) The situations in which the behavior occurs are relatively easy to define.
(4) The consequences of the behavior are relatively easy to describe.
(5) The behavior is relatively easy to reproduce by reinstating some or all aspects of the stimulus situation.
(6) The reproducibility of behavior and situation makes it

relatively easy to study the various levels of interaction between the stimuli and the responses that drive, and that correlate with, the complex behavior- situation relationship that characterizes the personality.

Self-Concept: Stable Constructs

Although by definition the shifty theory contains no static constructs for traits or states, at the individual level some stability of construct does emerge from careful analysis of data about the self-concept. The relatively stable constructs are:

(1) The compelling situation.
(2) The possible self.
(3) The working self.
(4) The essential audience.
(5) The personal scientist/theorist.

The Compelling Situation

As I get to know a client, I slowly begin using as summary terms some of the concepts and definitions from earlier personality theorists. But I refrain from using personality labels or trait labels until I have identified some clearly stable features in the client's behavior. I identify stable behavioral features by elucidating compelling situations in the individual's life. Earlier theorists have also attended to individually compelling situations. Murray's (1938) concept of "alpha press" and Cattell's (1965) concept of "erg" are based in part on the observation that for some people, certain specifiable environmental events or situations are particularly compelling. And these events or situations reliably result in a specific form of behavior. The particular behavior links up to a reciprocally determined sequence of interactions with the individual's environment. Such interactions will be examined in subsequent chapters.

Stressors can be equated with compelling situations. Some compelling situations are universally stressful (such as being involved in a train wreck), and some are highly individual (such as seeing a particular sort of facial expression on a man in a barroom). Some compelling situations are imposed on a person (such as getting multiple sclerosis or being injured in an accident), and others are sought after (such as participation in an arm-wrestling contest).

The universally compelling situations provide contexts in which the stable aspects of personality generally emerge. The more individually compelling situations can help distill stabilities from the shifty data.

In my clinical experience, I have repeatedly dealt with individuals who were coping with the most compelling situations of their lives (for example, the active man who suddenly becomes paralyzed through a spinal injury at T-2 after a fall). As mentioned above, the relationship between self and situation is clarified in these tragic conditions.

By putting clients in compelling situations in a test environment, some of the stable aspects of personality can be examined. We have examined thought and behavior patterns in response to a variety of moderate-stress but universally compelling situations. Two such situations in the laboratory are the pain caused by putting one's hand in ice water for 30 seconds and the excitement caused by being exposed to a fast-paced test of verbal and math skills.

Other workers who have emphasized the use of compelling situations in the assessment of personality include Wallace (1966). Rather than using the traditional method of assessing personality, which involves asking a subject to indicate how he or she typically responds to a particular situation – Wallace suggested that we set up combinations of situations and challenging instructions – asking the subject to indicate how capable he or she is of responding, or to say what sort of response would be shown if he or she tried as hard as possible. Willerman, Turner, and Peterson (1976) provided data supporting Wallace's suggestion. More recently, Seligman and his co-workers have developed powerful ideas and methods that examine responses (and expectancies regarding responses and outcomes) in compelling situations (e.g., Peterson and Seligman 1984). Observing the types, directions, and degrees of shifts in behavior and thought patterns during exposure to compelling conditions can tell us a great deal about an individual's personality.

On a general level, these ideas can be boiled down to two statements. The term biopsychosocial implies the existence of three domains; a compelling situation in any of these three domains – biological, psychological, or social – can be seen to influence the other two domains. Patterns with regard to how the three domains in an individual's life influence each other are helpful in formulating a theory of how the individual's personality operates.

The Possible Self

The possible future states of self that a person seriously considers provide keys to understanding that person. The work of Markus and Nurius (1986) indicates that the possible selves endorsed – and the probability attached to each possible self – during exposure to a compelling situation provide very powerful indicators about stable aspects of self-concept. In some ways we can say that personality is a shifty combination of traits and possible states; those states repeatedly seen in compelling situations are somewhat trait-like.

We are here considering the behavior of a specific group of individuals in compelling situations. The personalities of these individuals can be specified in terms of compelling conditions – those social situations in which they become violent – and their behavioral, thought, and biological processes in such situations can be examined. For these people, the possible self of specific interest is the feared possible self (as opposed to the hoped for possible self). This possible self is a particularly salient motivational force for violent clients. The subjective probabilities attached to the most feared self, along with the client's prior history of being in the state represented by that feared self, can also be examined. Finally, the role of negative reinforcement in developing the relationship between the feared possible self and the violent behavior patterns can be considered. This then is the utility of the relatively stable construct of the possible self.

The Working Self

The working self is the self-concept that is actually present *in vivo*, while the possible self may merge into the working self at one point and later disappear from use, only to emerge again. Markus and Nurius (1986) point out that there have been many failures to link self-concept to behavior, and they suggest a new strategy that does a much better job. Because their strategy represents an economical codification of some important aspects of my thinking and methodology, I will quote and paraphrase from them to establish a foundation for my use of several terms. As they see it self-concept is not a unitary entity. Self-concept is a system of "salient identities or self-schemas [possible selves] that lend structure and meaning to one's self-relevant experiences (page158)." These self-schemas are generalizations about the self derived from past experience, and they help one to integrate and explain one's own behavior. (Hebb in his "Essay On Mind" (1980) used some of these same concepts, particularly those pertaining to the development of schemas and the use of schemas in explaining one's own behavior.)

> Self-schema reflects a pervasive concern with a certain domain of behavior...self-schemas define a past and present self, but even more importantly they define a future, possible self. And it can be argued that this component is in fact the most significant aspect of the self-schema in shaping and fueling behavior (Markus and Nurius, 1986, page 158)... it is the possible self that puts the self into action (page 159)... To examine the potential utility of the notion of possible selves, we have proposed thinking not in terms of the self-concept but instead in terms of the working self-concept. The working self-concept is that set of self-conceptions that are presently accessible in thought and memory. It can be viewed as a continually active, shifting array of available self-knowledge. Not all knowledge is equally accessible for thinking about the self at any one time. The array changes depending on the contents of the prior working self-concept, on what self-conceptions have been activated by the immediate social circumstances, and on those self- conceptions that have been willfully invoked by the person in response to current experience (page 163).

Note how Markus and Nurius use the word shifting. They agree that self-concept is "shifty," and that it is frequently redefined. As they go on, Markus and Nurius point out that in two different compelling situations, two very different concepts of the working self may be active:

> These two sets may well contain the same self-schemas or core self-conceptions. Yet these core self-conceptions may be accompanied by views of the past, current, or future self that derive primarily from the immediate social circumstances. And it is these latter self-conceptions that will often

effectively compete with one's core self-conceptions for influence over the individual's prevailing affective and motivational states, current cognitive appraisals, and immediate actions (page 164).

The Essential Audience

An important force in the development of self-concept is the "essential audience," which serves a "critic function." This is the social aspect of the biopsychosocial model, as it pertains to the assumptions one makes regarding the way one looks to other people. Attending to this aspect is not new. For example, a recent paper (Loor and Wunderlich, 1986) describes development of a scale that measures perceived positive appraisal from "significant others." (I will refer to significant others as the essential audience and their perceived appraisal as the critic function.)

The role of the essential audience can be seen in several domains. The essential audience plays some role in the person's compilation of a subjective track record. The essential audience also plays a role in the probability a person attributes to various possible selves; for example, if a member of the essential audience predicts that one will end up in jail, this might become a powerfully negative possible self. The role of the essential audience (and its critic function) evolves in the early years of life in response to parental attention, and it represents the internalization of some aspects of parental attention.

The essential audience also plays a direct role in the formation of possible selves. Markus and Nurius have said that "self-schemas are constructed creatively and selectively from an individual's past experience in a particular domain." In past experiences, identifiable events and processes underlie and direct the development of the self-concept, including the possible selves. Some of these events and processes can be specified quite clearly and are shown in Chapter 4. The labels given a child by the parents are primary initial sources of possible selves. Also, negative reinforcement – as reflected in the history of many of our violent clients – is a notable and powerful source of the development of self-schemas that have manifestations in expectancies and dispositions. Most violent clients cite a specific experience (compelling situation) in childhood when they were being tormented and scared, and when they ended this suffering by a sudden outburst of violence. This somehow led to a realization that their repertoire contained a response that had a guaranteed positive outcome. Hence , a new possible self arises – the possible self who is powerful, and violent.   The figures in Chapter 14 elaborate on these observations and show the general sequence of events that leads to the development of the disposition to be violent.

The Personal Scientist/Theorist

Kelly (1955) and others have noted that we are all personal scientists in the sense that we work, and even struggle, to make sense of the world, of our impact on the world, and of our possible roles within the world. We are all personality theorists in the sense that we strive to develop lawlike statements about our own and other people's personalities. Among the most important motivations for these activities is our desire to increase our understanding and predictive ability regarding things that are important to us. Increasing our understanding and predictive ability in turn increases our sense of control over things that are important to us.

These theorizing activities take many forms and serve many purposes. In some situations, when we have a sense of ourselves, and of our values and wishes with regard to particular outcomes, we behave in accord with relatively describable goals, roles, and so forth. In other situations, our own behavior can be surprising to us, and thus we can become scientists and theorists working on the lifelong project of developing (or defending) a theory about ourselves. Sometimes we provide ourselves with raw data about ourselves, data that our scientist self gathers and that can be processed by our theorist self to develop a more detailed theory about ourselves. The suggestion of shifts in our point of view through this process is intentional. We shift from being an actor and a conscious role-player with defined goals, to being a reactor, to merely being an observed source of data; and we can shift back and forth again, from data source, to observer, to scientist, to theorist, to analyze and use new data.

Self Concept: Shifting Variables

The Binary Switch

The remarkable differences among people, and within people as time passes, represent a monumental challenge to the personal scientist/personality theorist. While some consistencies emerge in the behavior of people as time passes, the inconsistencies are many and salient. These inconsistencies extend even to the energy available to us for our own theorizing about the data from our own behavior. Sometimes we are active and clear-minded, and at other times we are passive, lazy or confused.

Meichenbaum (1980), agreeing with Goldfried et al. (1974) points out, "Because of the habitual nature of one's expectations or beliefs it is likely that the thinking processes and images become automatic and seemingly involuntary like most overlearned acts." I have observed that I, like others, often do act and think in ways that ignore data, reduce ambiguity, and reduce the number of opportunities available to make active choices and to act as a scientist or theorist about my own or other people's behaviors. One way to reduce ambiguity is to revert automatically to either-or propositions. The concept of a "binary switch" comes to mind when I think about these seemingly automatic, involuntary reactions.

This "binary switch" quality is easily observed in my clinical sample of individuals referred for outbursts of violent behavior. It is as if they have an either-or expectation of being insulted or being feared (two possibilities), and an either-or disposition of attacking or not attacking, (only two possible behavioral modes). Certain situations illuminate this binary quality in expectancy and disposition more dramatically than others. This observation with the violent clients is elaborated in later chapters (see especially Chapter 14); however, it is not hard to observe the occasional presence of such binary qualities in the expectations and dispositions of anyone.

The variability in the levels of energy available for or used in the theorizing endeavor seems to be accompanied by variation in the quality of that energy. At times we seem driven by negative, angry energy, and at other times we seem to express a more positive, happier energy. These levels and qualities of energy interact with the binary switch in ways that can be quite clearly specified for some individuals; these issues are addressed in Chapter 3.

The Quality of Internal Dialogue

Another area of variability among and within individuals is in the type, frequency, and role of their internal dialogue. In many of my violent clients, the internal dialogue seems to be (at best) monosyllabic and binary. In addition, the internal dialogue – if it does occur – often occurs *after* the overt behavior, so that environmental stimuli frequently lead directly to overt behavior, without time being taken for internal dialogue.

I am quite sure that most of my clients are different from those treated by Novaco (1975) and by most other authors of published accounts describing the assessment and treatment of violent individuals. In addition to demographic differences (mine have much lower average levels of education, and income), there are vast differences between the typical violent acts committed by my clients and those committed by Novaco's clients. For example, public fistfights were the rule among my clients, and more than half of my most recent 115 clients had beaten someone until they became unconscious during the year before treatment began. Novaco's clients were more likely to yell or push someone, and seemingly only one of 34 had a fistfight in public. But the most important difference seems to be in the richness of their internal dialogue and the related opportunity to pause and consider before striking out. With my clients, I had to work hard to move them from the binary switch mode of expectancy and disposition to a different mode, to get them to slow down and process environmental events, to reflect, and to consider a variety of possible expectations, dispositions, responses and possible outcomes.

My own thinking on internal dialogue, and indeed on the issue of all people being personal scientists/theorists, has been influenced by a number of others in addition to Hebb. These include William James, George Kelly and Joseph Rychlak. Recent writings by currently active investigators show some overlapping influences. For example, Meichenbaum (1980) says:

> Imagine yourself attending your junior-high-school reunion twenty years after graduation. Could you guess what your classmates are like? Why else do we attend such reunions? Perhaps we are all personologists at heart! As Block (1971) stated in describing such a hypothetical reunion:

> In the passage of almost a generation, the capriciousness of adolescence has been left and lives have taken their essential form and direction. There are the usual indicators of the passage of time – the formerly lissome and lithe may now be pudgy and stiff; the great adolescent dreams of glamour and omnipotence largely have been deflated by reality; for most, money, comfort, and status have become the order of the day (pages 306 and 307)...

> How you observe and describe the behavioral changes and constancies in your fellow classmates at that 20-year junior-high-school reunion will be influenced by the implicit theory of personality you hold (page 309).

These engaging quotes from Meichenbaum raise two subtle issues that I must comment on. First, notice that the data being processed by the personal scientist/theorist are provided both by behavior of self and by behavior of others. Second, not only does the point of view thereby shift, but a continuing transaction among data sources is considered. While other personality theorists have examined these two issues, the examination has generally been cumbersome and long-winded. Perhaps we can see Meichenbaum's words and example as providing a reference point to help bring such subtle and complex considerations into a clearer focus.

Summary

At this stage, we need all the clarity of focus we can manage. This chapter on a shifty personality theory has probably proved the point that certainty and stability are elusive in this work. But at least we can clarify the focus. To that end, here is a summary of what we've covered so far of my shifty personality theory:

(1) A good personality theory will prevent clinician and client from being overwhelmed by behavioral and situational diversity.
(2) Personality is a description of specific behavior patterns in specific situations.
(3) A shifty personality theory is, by definition, only a theory of one person's behavior.
(4) A shifty personality theory can be developed, over time, as one gains experience with a particular individual. It is built up from minitheories developed by observing interactions between that person and certain specific environmental events.
(5) A good approach to shifty personality theorizing is to make use of a "life chart" that relates important events in a person's life to the various biological, psychological, and social experiences of that person's life.

(6)   Careful attention to naturally occurring and universally compelling situations, such as a trauma or the death of a family member, will help develop a personality theory that encompasses some of the stable aspects of the individual's personality.

(7)   Examination of behavior in replicable, universally compelling situations (such as evaluation of reactivity to a standardized stressor) will also help clarify aspects of the individual's personality.

(8)   The identification of compelling situations that are idiosyncratic to the client and that interact with reliable patterns of thought (e.g., expectancies and dispositions) and behavior will also help in development of a personality theory.

(9)   The three facets of the biopsychosocial model (bio, psycho, social) imply various ways of influencing the individual's personality; monitoring of relationships among compelling situations – in each of the three domains – and of patterns of change in the other two domains are part and parcel of the data from which a shifty personality theory is formulated.

(10) The working self concept is a key, and the shifts – from day to day and from situation to situation – in the working self should be encompassed by a shifty personality theory.

(11) The social facet of the biopsychosocial model is made clear by the concept of essential audience and its critic function; these should be carefully considered as having origins both in early experience and in the present social circumstance.

(12) The formulation of a shifty personality theory should enlist the client as a personal scientist/theorist. Training the client in development of conceptual models and in the use of various points of view is a worthwhile activity, though some clients will be more amenable to this than others.

(13) The binary switch concept should be carefully considered when it applies to manifestation of problem behavior.

(14) Developing, testing and practicing specific forms of internal dialogue should be involved in the development of a personality theory, as well as in therapy for many clients.

In clinical settings, developing the shifty personality theory is a joint effort involving both client and therapist; both the activity and the result can be expected to facilitate the processes of assessment and therapy. Both client and therapist should be braced for the continuing transactional and shifting nature of personality – because a personality theory is never finished.

3 : Biological Variables in Personality

In Meichenbaum's engaging discussion of the quote in the preceding Chapter, he noted four major processes that influence the theorizing activity:

(1) Cognitive structures
(2) Internal dialogue
(3) Behavioral acts
(4) Evaluation of outcomes

Meichenbaum omitted biological concepts. While he did not need the biological dimension for his example, biological concepts are necessary for comprehending the personality of a violent client in a compelling situation.

Biological variables are often omitted in the personality theory literature. Perhaps this correlates with the fact that extremely compelling or stressful situations are not often considered by personality theorists. The interactions among biological variables, a stressful situation, and a relative absence of internal dialogue are illustrated by an event in the life of one of my violence-prone clients.

This man attended a reunion, and after most of the attendees had consumed at least one glass of beer and done some vigorous dancing, one of his classmates greeted my client's fiancée with (my client thought) too much enthusiasm. The classmate kissed the fiancée on the cheek. Immediately, while the kiss was still going on, my client punched his classmate in the face. At this point (according to the testimony of the client and his fiancée) the client began to weep uncontrollably. The story continues with complications and provides a rich tapestry of interaction between biological variables and the reactions of one who made scant use of internal dialogue.

The eventual reconstruction of this particular scene in a role playing situation, with biological variables being monitored, permitted the client and therapist to develop some understanding about the relationship among biological variables, expectancies, dispositions, and behavioral acts. They were also able to lay the foundation for internal dialogue in future situations of a similar sort.

The Sympathetic Nervous System: An Emotional Fire in the Boiler

A discussion of the sympathetic nervous system, the "emotional fire in the boiler," will help illustrate the interplay between cognitive processes, such as internal dialogue and expectancy, and emotional or arousal processes.

Most readers are probably well aware of some aspects of central nervous system function, but much less aware of the functions of the autonomic nervous system. The autonomic nervous system (ANS) innervates heart, viscera, smooth muscles, blood vessels, and glands. The ANS has two divisions – the sympathetic nervous system (SNS), which arouses or activates, and the parasympathetic nervous system (PNS), which generally functions to quiet the target organs and actually counteracts many of the SNS functions (but often only after a long time and sometimes only weakly). Many measures have been used to monitor SNS activity. Two of these reflect activities of the SNS that are not modulated by the PNS – these are skin conductance (or skin resistance) and peripheral blood flow. Years of monitoring these and other biological processes have convinced me that the SNS deserves the label of "emotional fire in the boiler." Other workers, including Brooks and Lange (1982), have noted the modulating and level-setting functions of the ANS. Bannister (1982) noted that all organs and processes in the body are influenced by the ANS.

The most dramatic results that I have obtained have come from monitoring skin conductance level. With a particular set of instruments, my colleagues and I have repeatedly observed that skin conductance provides an index of emotional arousal that correlates in time course and magnitude very closely with subjective sensations of emotional arousal. For example, in a sample of 50 consecutive clients, we have uniformly observed reliable correlations between skin conductance level and a two-minute discussion of the client's most recent experience of anger. We placed this discussion in between two five-minute periods of relaxation. Specifically, the magnitude of skin conductance elevation and the time course of development and recovery of this change corresponded with the period of discussion and with the sensations of emotional arousal. We have not observed this level of correspondence between arousing discussions and other biological variables (such as peripheral blood flow, heart rate, or forehead EMG).

In using these instruments with more than 100 violent clients, I have never seen an exception to the following statement:

> SNS arousal, as indexed by skin conductance, correlates with descriptions of situations that provoked anger and descriptions of anger-related violent behavior.

The following generalizations are also supported by our observations:

(1) Descriptions of other arousing experiences (for example, humorous occasions) also correlate with SNS arousal, but less reliably.

(2) Whenever other indicators of arousal (facial expression, tone of voice) are present, skin conductance is always elevated.

(3) Even when there are no other objective indications of arousal, but when a subjective report of emotional arousal is given, arousal is tracked reliably by skin conductance level.

For the purposes of this chapter, consider the SNS as an "emotional fire in the boiler." It sets the levels of many other bodily processes. This level-setting function results in shifting of the probability of perceptual, cognitive, and overt behaviors. (The specificity of these relationships will be demonstrated in later chapters.)

Central Motive State

While some functions of the ANS are actually patterned, or differentiated, and lateralized (Wallin and Fagius, 1986; Lane and

Schwartz, 1987, Ekman, 1983), here the relatively undifferentiated arousing function is the most important contribution of the SNS. For the differentiation, direction, or quality of mood, we must look for interplay between the ANS and the central nervous system. A convenient summary concept for such an interplay between the central and the autonomic nervous systems is Bindra's (1974) concept of "central motive state." This concept is related to earlier notions such as "drive," "need," and "press," but in Bindra's theory the logical consistency and heuristic power are very appealing. Central motive state is shifty, reciprocally determined, and determining, and it is influenced by the ANS (both the SNS and the PNS), by endocrine, digestive, and other internal processes, and by the interaction of these processes with environmental events. In turn, these environmental events take on incentive value as a function of their interaction with the central motive state.

For this discussion, the central motive state can be seen as a central integrator or registry, while the SNS functions as the level-setting "emotional fire in the boiler". The central motive state serves to interpret global ANS, endocrine, and other variables that contribute to psychological entities typically grouped under the heading of "mood," while the SNS emotional fire in the boiler is both a level-indicator and a level-setter. The intensity of the fire in the boiler will thus be accurately reflected by skin conductance, while the particular direction, quality, or mood of the central motive state will be reflected by overt behavior (or by a combination of behavior with several physiological indicators, as has been demonstrated by Ekman, 1983).

Central Motive State, Working Self, Personal Theorist and Point of View

The central motive state is also helpful in considering, or describing the forces in play at any moment in the behavior of a person. As mentioned above, the construct of the working self refers to the aspects of the self-concept that are functional at any given moment. The working self-concept in any specific environment includes several related sets of expectancies – including expectancies about these particular stimuli or stressors, available responses, and likely outcome of each response. In accord with the definitions and concepts discussed earlier regarding point of view, I will now attempt to define and describe a few ideas about the interfaces between personal theorizing, current working self, and central motive state.

At almost any waking moment, an individual may be said to have available to him or her a sense of existing, of being alive, of being a self in an environment, of being an agent – at least in the sense being able to shift attention (point of view) to various aspects of the environment. Which particular aspects of the self or the environment attention is shifted to – will be partly a function of the central motive state. Central motive state will cause some aspects of the environment to become incentive stimuli (i.e., stimuli that are sought after or avoided) that would otherwise have been ignored. This central motive state may be determined in part by aspects of self-concept, including feared future possible selves. As mentioned above, central motive state is also influenced by SNS arousal. In turn, the particular behavioral acts that are selected are also influenced by working self-concept, internal dialogue, past conditioning, and expectancies and response dispositions. These interactions are depicted in Figure 3.1.

An example of how these various features work together is provided by an elaboration of some of the aspects of the kissing episode described above. My client had a history of being humiliated by older brothers and neighbors, and his first girlfriend had been taken away from him by his older brother. He had developed an expectancy of certain kinds of humiliation. A salient experience with the termination of humiliation (negative reinforcement) coming about as a function of his physically exploding and hitting someone (negatively-reinforced behavior) had led to a very strong disposition to hit or explode whenever he was humiliated. This disposition was more evident when he had consumed some alcohol. Thus the emotional fire in the boiler and central motive state, with attendant expectations and dispositions, led to a response to this incentive event--a response that could have been predicted with some knowledge of this client's background and apparent concepts of self. The feared possible self – humiliated loser, unlovable person, someone without a girlfriend – appeared to be a salient motivator.

The delineation of all aspects and forces in this particular situation would be very difficult. However, we often work with clients to develop a model of relationships among a compelling situation, a working self-concept (including possible selves), and biological variables in order to see how various settings of parameters and points of view can influence behavior. My colleagues and I have occasionally attempted to use computer-based, systems-dynamics modeling of the forces acting in a specific situation experienced by a particular client. We used a format in which the client interacts directly with the computer to adjust parameters of situation, reaction, and so forth, to see if this would be helpful with development of more adaptive internal dialogue, and with the development of a personal theorist point of view. As far as we were able to determine, the computer-based, systems-dynamics modeling was not as good for these purposes as are the more simple models shown in Chapters 8, 9, and 12. However, a few clients have been able to profit from participation in a long-term exercise involving such complicated modeling activity.

With one client (Mr. B described in Chapter 13), we developed a model of his responses to a compelling situation which involved looking out of his window and seeing a snowplow hit his car and move it a few feet. His reactions and the events of the next hour were diagramed. He collaborated with us in every aspect, filling in the various details of events at each level shown in Table 1.1 in Chapter 1. He went on to develop two careful drawings of his own mini-models, depicting the time course and the variables involved in the rise and fall of his fire in the boiler, how these interacted with his working self-concept, his internal dialogue, and the responses of the snowplow driver. (It is worth noting that this particular client is highly intelligent and well-educated.)

To illustrate some of the individual differences involved in this level of processing, consider Mr. D (who will reappear later). While we were developing the data for the systems dynamics depiction of this episode, Mr. D, another intelligent violent client was present and was asked to participate. Mr. D participated only passively and expressed no real interest in the project. He was a client we knew well, and we were able to develop a tentative systems-dynamics representation of one of his own episodes of violent behavior. However, it rapidly became clear that the computer modeling strategy was wasted on this individual. He could understand the complexity, but the theorizing style and point of view were not interesting, motivating, or helpful to him. Furthermore, it became clear that even the first individual was better served by a more simple diagram, such as is shown in the less complex Figures 13.13-13.18 in Chapter 13.

The simple notions of emotional fire in the boiler and mood, or central motive state, were helpful with both clients. The client who was not interested in the modeling activity described above was interested in the one-sentence rationale that summarized the following more elaborate concept:

> The level of the emotional fire in your boiler, and the reactivity of the emotional fire in your boiler, as well as your mood, are determined by your attitudes toward yourself and toward the situations you find yourself in. Part of your job is to lower the level of the fire in your boiler and to lower the reactivity of the fire to situations that have previously caused you to become violent; another part of your job is to control your attitude. A way to do this is to attend to the level of the fire in your boiler and to signs of a sudden increase in the fire. Whenever the fire is hot – or getting hotter – you must say out loud, "I'm upset," and then you must simultaneously begin the tasks of quieting yourself and working toward developing an attitude of thoughtful problem-solving, while actively avoiding the old attitudes that have led so often to violent behavior.

While this statement is long and complicated, repeated reminders about and rehearsal of the simple formula embodied in the following short sentence have proven helpful with even the most primitive and impaired clients:

> When you notice the fire in the boiler say, 'I'm upset' and then quickly start using your relaxation response.

How we use this simple formula illustrates the bare bones of a wide variety of clinical applications of the shifty personality theory. Clients easily come to understand, and recognize in themselves, the relationships among the fire in the boiler and their various biopsychosocial problems. In fact, if there is a common cornerstone to the shifty personality theory developed for each client this is it: *The fire in the boiler has to be acknowledged and consciously monitored and modulated by the client if he or she is to improve.*

This monitoring and modulating of the fire in the boiler actually implies a wide rage of activities – depending on the particular client. For those such as Mr. B, who responded well to a complex systems-dynamics model, the whole range of forces can be considered: the level and reactivity of the boiler, or sympathetic nervous system, the registration of mood, or central motive state, and the reciprocal interactions of these with the working self-concept, with overt behavior and with the environment. The rapid shifts in point of view that were possible for this personal theorist made such thinking quite easy. He developed a rich internal dialogue and moved himself quickly away from the binary switch mode of reacting that had characterized his behavior at the time of referral. On the other hand, Mr. D seemed to be stuck at the binary-switch level. His internal dialogue, if it was present, was only monosyllabic, and it was usually so slow to occur that it didn't happen until after he had already become violent. The simple sentence described above worked to move him from the extremely rapid binary switch mode by an external version of internal dialogue (saying out loud "I'm upset" whenever he notices the fire in his boiler at a high level, or notices it rising). This simple formula led to immediate changes in his behavior outside of the treatment setting and laid the foundation for the development of some internal dialogue and some, albeit primitive, alteration in cognitive-perceptual function.

Summary

The constructs and variables considered in this and the previous chapter are shown in Figure 3.1. While I rarely use figures of this sort in direct work with clients, variations of this figure and sections of it can be helpful. (Chapter 13 contains an example of the use of this figure with a violent client; see Figure 13.14.) For our current purposes, this figure summarizes this and the previous chapter and the general approach to shifty personality theorizing. Once again, the common foundation of all shifty personality theories for the clients I work with is the emotional fire in the boiler. This fundamental force must be constantly monitored and modulated if the client is to progress.

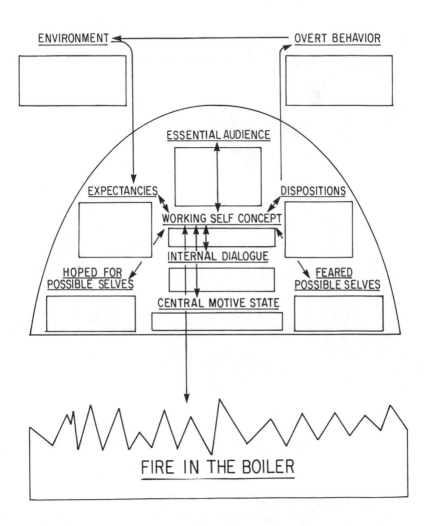

Figure 3.1. *Pictorial summary of constructs and variables involved in shifty personality theory.*

Part Two

Lessons from the Family

4 : Families as Mutual Control Systems

In this chapter, I will present some theoretical notions about families. I will emphasize the relationship between parental attention and the development of social incentives. My main assumption is that the management by parents of their attention to their children is a key to the children's later sense of themselves (their self-concept), their responsiveness to all incentives, and their general mode of adjustment to the adult world.

In her classic book *For Your Own Good,* Alice Miller (1984) points out many problems and hidden cruelties in childrearing and sees these as the primary roots of violence. She concentrates most on psychological cruelties, but also addresses the issue of physical abuse by parents of their children. She equates any form of physical punishment of children with abuse, and she does not accept the differentiation of spanking from abusive beating. She cites examples of physical and psychological violence being perpetuated from generation to generation, and she makes a very strong case that Adolph Hitler was abused by his parents in ways that had much to do with his devastatingly violent behaviors as an adult.

Parental Attention

Miller eloquently illustrates the power of parental attention and gives numerous examples of parental attention evolving into a very negative "essential audience." For example, she traces the development of parental coercive tactics into a power so great that a brief disapproving glance from the parent causes the child to feel both transparent and guilty. She convincingly explains how, in some cases, these tactics of management of parental attention can lead to the eventual development of psychotic paranoid behavior (see especially, pages 4- 6).

Miller says she values any possible methods of helping children to see themselves as agents and as persons to be taken seriously, but she avoids offering specific advice on what methods might be helpful. Instead, she sees it as her task to "expose the roots of hatred" (page 9).

In an afterword to her second edition (1984), Miller says that the knowledge she has offered us "concerns every single one of us, and – if disseminated widely enough – should lead to fundamental changes in society; above all, to a halt in the blind escalation of violence."

Miller's essential message can be summarized in a few words. The mere use of physical punishment does not itself eventually cause a child to become violent; but the cruel and unpredictable use of parental power, in the form of physical or psychosocial punishment and control, is very likely to lead to later problems, many of which involve violence. While Miller does not specify methods, she does specify objectives: "For their development, children need respect and protection of adults who take them seriously, love them, and honestly help them to become oriented to the world" (Afterword, 1984).

Miller describes many wrong-minded attempts to specify guidelines, formats, and programs for child-rearing and pedagogy. She scorns them all and illustrates their sometimes subtle abusive features. There are many published programs for child-rearing that Miller did not mention, including my own (1974). This chapter presents that program as a possible means of reaching Miller's objective of producing a fundamental change in society that will help halt the blind escalation of violence.

Mutual Control Systems

Skinner (1961) noted that all social organizations can be characterized as mutual control systems, with control being exercised upon, as well as being exercised by, each member of an organization.

Individuals can be seen as members of many mutual control systems, including their families, their work environment, and the various levels of the society in which they live. Within each of these systems, the individual's behavior is controlled by a characteristic set of categories, sources, and schedules of reinforcement.[1]

In this context, development from infancy to adulthood can easily be seen as involving a progression through various types of mutual control systems and various levels of participation in each control system. Furthermore, any mutual control system can be characterized by an implied and more-or-less concise contract that sets forth the privileges, responsibilities, and reinforcement contingencies for each member of the system. The laws in adult society can be seen as components of an explicit contract, and in some occupational systems contracts are explicit. But explicit contracts are relatively rare at other levels of society. In fact, most other systems, including family, demand inferences on the part of their members about the nature of an implied contract.

The implied nature of most contracts can be seen as a source of confusion about privilege and responsibility and, in turn, as a source of many developmental problems. The case has been made that some of the problems of adolescence are due to the increasing ambiguity of the adolescent's changing role (privileges and respon-sibilities) in the family as he or she progresses toward adulthood. I believe that occurrence of these problems can be decreased, and the eventual transfer into other control systems can be facilitated, if family members develop an explicit contract (and modify the contract as expectations change) instead of relying on the implied (and often inconsistent) contract.

Reinforcement and Learning

A number of attempts to reach this general objective have been based on Skinner's plan (1948, 1971) for the redesign of society. This plan involves careful management of positive reinforcement (reward or "good things") and the minimum use of negative reinforcement (threat of, or delivery of, punishment or "bad things"). We now have a large body of data with which to evaluate

[1] Instead of the term reinforcement, I would have preferred to use the term incentive stimulus throughout; but most readers are likely to be unfamilar with incentive theory. Incentive theory was described in detail by Bindra (1974) and is first used in the present chapter to deal with interactions between parental attention and self-esteem. Following this introduction, I will assume that the reader understands that, in the rest of this book, I equate positive reinforcement with appetitive or positive incentive stimuli, and negative reinforcement with aversive or negative incentive stimuli.

the impact of these procedures. Results with the very early phases of development and with regressed and retarded populations are encouraging (Kazdin and Bootzin, 1972, Atthowe, 1973). Results with later phases of development and with subjects who are not retarded or regressed are not as encouraging. Among the problems encountered in the use of such programs with relatively normal populations (in both therapeutic and communal settings) are:

(1) High administrative costs of positive reinforcement schemes
(2) Eventual necessity of using powerful negative reinforcers to prevent system failure (Kinkade, 1973)
(3) Mismatch problem (or sequencing failure) when a person leaving such a program reenters the real world as it now is, not yet redesigned in accord with Skinner's plan.

An essential aspect of the mismatch problem is the difference between the reinforcement schedules typical of Skinner's program and the real world. The Skinnerian system carefully manages and makes maximum use of positive reinforcement and attempts to make minimal use of negative reinforcement. On the other hand, the schedules of reinforcement in the real adult world, as it is now, can be characterized as follows:

(1) Salient positive reinforcement is usually unreliable and/or separated from salient positively reinforcable behavior by long intervals (that is, it is on variable low-ratio [e.g., 30:1] or long-interval schedules)
(2) Salient negative reinforcement is usually reliable and/or separated from salient negatively reinforcable behavior by short intervals (that is, it is on fixed high-ratio [e.g., 1:1] or short-interval schedules).

Skinner's remarks suggest that he would agree with this characterization of the present real-world reinforcement schedules (1961, page 542; 1971 page 57).

Additional support for this point of view comes from a classic paper by White (1976), who summarized data from a number of studies concerning the presentation to students, in grades 1 through 12, of signals categorized as "positive reinforcers" and "negative reinforcers." Results showed a shift toward an increasing percentage of negative reinforcement after the second grade. Additional support comes from an article (*Tharp and Gallimore, 1976*) describing the coaching behavior of a famous and successful basketball coach, John Wooden at UCLA. Results showed that the coach was giving his players about twice as much negative-incentive information as positive-incentive information. If these character- izations of the reinforcement schedules in the real world are accurate, I would argue that both educational and remedial systems should be organized to facilitate the individual's transition to this state of affairs.

The Development of Self-Concept

Another important objective of these educational and remedial systems should be the development in the individual of the concept of self as an agent capable of contracting with other agents for the operation of mutual control systems. The basic idea underlying this objective has been put forth by Skinner and others, including Miller (1984), who uses very different terminology to make this same general point. The optimal level of participation in a mutual control system ranges from informed and consenting participation in system operation to active participation in system design and evolution. To reach this level, a person must develop:

(1) A sense of self
(2) Some understanding of the mutuality of control in the systems in which one participates
(3) A concept of the examinable, negotiable, and relatively arbitrary nature of contracts (or of the objectives and operational details of the control systems)
(4) An impression of oneself as an active and respected agent in examining and negotiating the contracts for the mutual control systems in which one participates.

These notions touch on many important issues, such as questions regarding determinism versus freedom of choice and the presumed existential states of "object" and "being"; however, I will ignore these in order to make clear the operational details of my position and proposals. An additional objective of these educational and remedial systems should be the development of self-esteem, or a positive self-concept or "self-theory" (Epstein, 1973, 1980). (While this objective relates closely to the development of the concept of the self as a contracting agent (point 4 above), it can also involve a very different set of features.)

As discussed in earlier chapters, *self-concept*, is a term for summarizing many effects of an individual's reinforcement history and for his or her current self-labeling and self-reinforcing behavior (Bandura, 1969). In terms of incentive theory (Bindra, 1974), the development of self-esteem or self-concept has several major stages. In the first stage, parental attention becomes a strong conditioned incentive stimulus. This happens when the infant learns the correlation between parental attention and various unconditioned incentive stimuli like food and warmth. In earliest infancy, deviations from a homeostatic, or balanced, and comfortable state are the primary unconditioned aversive incentive stimuli; reinstatement of the homeostatic state involves the primary unconditioned appetitive incentive stimuli. The repeated pairing of parental presence with the return to homeostatic state attaches, or conditions, appetitive incentive stimulus power to parental presence (see Figure 4. 1). This notion can easily be supported from various sources; for example; Fitzgerald and Brackbill (1976) described a number of remarkable examples of conditioning in human beings at very early ages. Additional support, admittedly of a tangential nature, come from an observation I made (1964) of a cat which had learned to press a wheel in order to obtain milk. During extinction this cat pressed more when I was in the room than when I was out of the room, suggesting that I had become a conditioned appetitive incentive stimulus. From such evidence, I concluded that the very young infant is able to form the same sort of association.

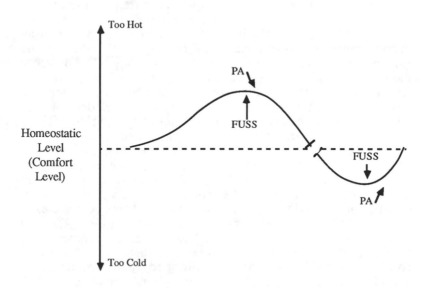

Repeated Pairing of PA with the Return to a
Comfortable Level is the first case of pairing a
previously neutral stimulus PA with a positive incentive
or "Reward"

Figure 4.1. *Parental attention becomes the first conditioned incentive stimulus.*

The conditioned incentive power of parental attention is observable very early in life and is sometimes awc-inspiring (Kolata, 1987). In fact, I have often likened this power to an overwhelming addiction (see figure 4.2). I expect that the data and examples presented here will support this analogy. The power of the essential audience (as discussed in Chapters 2 and 3) comes from the conditioned incentive power of parental attention, and the critic function of the essential audience depends for its development on subtleties of the management of parental attention. These features are spelled out in the following paragraphs.

The relationship between parental presence and various unconditioned incentive stimuli becomes more complex as the child grows older (see Figure 4.3). For the fortunate infant, somewhere between the ages of 3 and 12 months, appetitive and aversive qualities of parental behavior and related variables become clearly distinguishable and easily predictable (see Figure 4.4). For example, messages in the "You're OK" category become conditioned appetitive incentive stimuli because they are so frequently correlated with delivery of unconditioned appetitive incentive stimuli. (See Harris, 1967, for an elaboration of the "OK" terminology and Bandura, 1969, for a discussion of social learning theory.) Messages in the "You're not OK" category become conditioned aversive incentive stimuli because they are correlated with unconditioned aversive incentive stimuli (such as pain, or deprivation). The developmental course of the conditioned incentive power of parental attention determines the success or failure of its later subdivision (or discrimination) into positive and negative qualities (see Figure 4.5). This course also determines the success or failure of the eventual transfer to nonparents of the conditioned incentive power of various qualities of attention. In other words, this course lays the foundation for later responses to social reinforcement. And this foundation constitutes the general self-concept or self-theory (see Figures 4.6 and 4.7), including the associated expectancies and dispositions. (See Figures 4.8a through 4.8c).

By its association with almost all good
experiences in early months of life "PA" gains great
incentive power - one could say that the infant becomes
<u>"ADDICTED" TO PA</u>

Figure 4.2. *Addiction to parental attention.*

PARENTAL ATTENTION

is often paired with both
verbal and non verbal behavior of Parents - these
behaviors also become
CONDITIONED INCENTIVE STIMULI.

These stimuli include labels of the child and/or
child's behavior as "OK"

Figure 4.3. *Generalization of incentive power of parental attention.*

PARENTAL ATTENTION

is later subdivided into "OK" and "Not OK" categories

Figure 4.4. *Discrimination-subdivision of parental attention.*

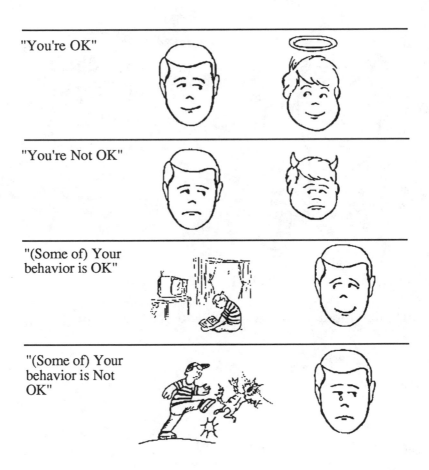

Figure 4.5. *Further discrimination-subdivision of parental attention.*

WHEN PARENTS MANAGE ATTENTION WELL THE CHILD'S SELF-CONCEPT IS -

"I'm OK

-Even if some of my behavior is Not OK"

Figure 4.6. *Outcome when parents manage attention well.*

WHEN PARENTS MANAGE ATTENTION BADLY
THE CHILD'S SELF-CONCEPT MAY BE -

"I'm Not OK

- No matter if some of my behavior is OK

- everyone still knows I'm Not OK"

Figure 4.7. *Outcome when parents manage attention badly.*

A POOR SELF-CONCEPT CAN PRODUCE
UNUSUAL RESPONSES - EVEN TO MESSAGES
INTENDED AS REWARDS.

Figure 4.8a. *A poor self concept can produce unusual responses.*

OR

Figure 4.8b. *A poor self concept can produce unusual responses (guilt).*

OR

Figure 4.8c. *A poor self concept can produce unusual responses (fear).*

Summary

In summary, I have argued the following points:

(1) Families are mutual control systems
(2) The family system should be leveled or sequenced so that the older children can transfer successfully to the control systems of the real adult world
(3) Children should see themselves capable of evaluating and influencing the systems in which they participate
(4) The development of self-esteem, or a positive self-concept, and of later responses to social reinforcement, are profoundly influenced by children's experiences with parental attention.

5 : The Family Optimization Program

With my colleagues, I have developed a program to assist families in optimizing the participation of their verbal children in society's mutual control systems. In this chapter I will describe this program and its application in two kinds of families – families that seem normal and families that are troubled.

The family optimization program can be used as a prophylactic, or optimizing, strategy for "normal" families, or it can be used to treat troubled families. The overall objective of the program is to promote a wealth-sharing team concept and to give both greater and more explicit control to the children than is typical in North American society.

Primary components of the program are:

(1) A specific family-unit contract regarding the duties and privileges of all members
(2) A method for systematizing parental attention
(3) A method for systematizing, monitoring, and eventually matching positive and negative reinforcement (rewards and punishments in parental language) to real-world schedules.

Application With Normal Families

I will first describe the methods we used and the results we obtained in implementing the program with five normal families. (Many dozens of families have used this program before and since its testing with these five families.) General features of the program will be described, and some data presented, but I will omit the specifics of baseline procedures, operationalization, and parent training, in part because these varied so much from family to family.

The Contract

First, whenever possible, we gathered the family together and discussed the general idea of the family unit as a team. We emphasized the importance of all members knowing their privileges and responsibilities and of refraining from behaviors detrimental to themselves or to other family members. A contract was developed as follows:

(1) The parents and children listed the responsibilities and privileges of each family member.
(2) The parents and children listed any behaviors of any family member (including themselves) that bothered them or other family members.
(3) The parents and the children listed the rewards and punishments currently used in the family.
(4) We discussed and edited these lists in collaboration with the family.
(5) The lists were made into a contract (a sample contract for a 9-year-old boy is shown in Table 5.1).

Parents' responsibilities were understood to include earning money, preparing most meals, and being systematic and self-controlled in monitoring behavior and in delivering rewards and punishments. Parents also had the responsibility to be the leaders and primary decision-makers and to be evenhanded in discussing problems and progress, as well as in reconsidering contract details at regular intervals. The children, as developing members of the team, also had responsibilities, and certain of their behaviors were to be monitored by the parents. Children would receive some of their usual rewards and punishments in accord with the contract. (See Table 5.1)

Table 5.1
Sample Contract for a 9-Year-Old Boy in a Two-Child Family

Tommy's Responsibilities	Unacceptable Behaviors
1. Brush Teeth	1. Hitting sister
2. Make bed	2. Destroying others' belongings
3. Clean up room	3. Teasing sister
4. Feed dog	4. Untidiness
5. Get along well with sister	5. Disobeying
6. Complete homework	6. Arguing
7. Go to bed at 8:00	7. Irritating

Examples of Privileges and Sanctions for Tommy:

1. If Tommy gets two "G's" on any one day, he may watch two hours of T.V. programs of his choice the following night.
2. If Tommy gets only one "G" on any day, he may watch one hour of a T.V. program of his choice the following night.
3. If Tommy gets a total of 14 "G's" in any week he receives $1.40 that Saturday; he may pick his choice of dessert for two suppers in the following week; he may stay up until 9:00 on Saturday and Sunday nights.
4. If Tommy gets only 10 "G's" in any week he receives $1.00 that Saturday and he may pick his choice of dessert for one supper the following week.
5. If Tommy gets only 7 "G's" or less in any week, he will not go bowling with Dad on Saturday morning; he may not watch T.V. all of the following week; he may not get to pick his choice of dessert; and he gets one dime for each "G" received in that week.
6. If Tommy gets 5 marks for unacceptable behavior on any one day he is given a spanking immediately after he receives the 5th mark.
7. Whenever a mark for unacceptable behavior is entered on the chart, Tommy is notified about it, and whenever possible this will be the only attention Tommy receives for the unacceptable behavior.
8. No matter how many marks of any category Tommy gets, he can spend time alone with one of his parents each morning.

Signed and agreed upon by:

_____   _____   _____

Throughout, the complex mutuality of control within the family team was emphasized, as were two obligations of all members: (1) to be aware of the necessity for changes in the contract (such as permitting increases in responsibility and privilege as children grow), and (2) to take an active role in considering and discussing possible changes.

Systematic Parental Attention

We systematized some parental attention by means of a very simple procedure. Every morning at breakfast, for the five days of the working week, one child was in a separate room (such as a den) with the father alone, and without sibling(s) or mother present. This lasted for about 45 minutes, and in a two-child family each child would receive father's attention every other day. On alternate days, the child would be in the kitchen with the mother (receiving some of her attention). This can be seen as programmed parental attention that is not contingent upon bad or good behavior of the children. Parental attention was paired with part of the daily ritual to ensure its occurrence, and was intended to partially satisfy the children's urge for (addiction to) individual parental attention.

Our technique for systematizing punishment and reward was more complex. The family taped to the kitchen wall a chart on graph paper with days of the month blocked out on it (sample charts are shown in Table 5.2). Each incident of contractually proscribed detrimental (unacceptable) behavior was immediately entered on the chart in the form of the first letter of the descriptive term (e.g., a tantrum was denoted by a T, hitting by an H). The letter G denoted good behavior. Marks for unacceptable behavior were entered at the time the behavior occurred, and the Gs were entered during a review session the following morning. The maximum possible number of Gs per day was two; two Gs were given when a child had indulged in no unacceptable behaviors on the previous day. Two Gs implied that the child had met all responsibilities. A child who indulged in one unacceptable behavior on the previous day got only one G, and if unacceptable behavior occurred, two or more times he or she got no Gs. The parents were instructed to complete the morning review session quickly after giving praise for Gs and then to have a general discussion with the child over breakfast. This discussion was to be unrelated to unacceptable behavior and was to be used as a specific time for the child to receive individual positive attention.

Table 5.2
Sample Charts

	Week #	Sat	Sun	Mon	Tues	Wed	Thur	Fri	# Bad Behaviors/ # Good Behaviors	Weekly Income
Tommy	1	HDD	HG	HG	DG	GG	DH	GG	8/7	.30
	2	TG	HH	UD	UG	GG	GG	DG	7/7	.35
	3									
	4									
	5									
	6									

	Week #	Sat	Sun	Mon	Tues	Wed	Thur	Fri	# Bad Behaviors/ # Good Behaviors	Weekly Income
Susan	1	TG	GG	TAU	DG	TTDU	TG	UG	11/6	.05
	2	DG	AID	UG	GG	GG	TG	GG	6/9	.60
	3									
	4									
	5									
	6									

Note that the reinforcements were delivered in accord with the real-world schedules mentioned earlier, with negative reinforcers on a high-ratio, short-interval schedule and with certain salient positive reinforcers on a low-ratio, long-interval schedule. Note also that this scheme is very different from the typical "token economy" approach (Atthowe, 1973). The scheme is in fact opposite to the token approach in some respects (such as attention to rapid delivery of negative incentives and long delays of material and nonroutine positive incentives).

All the marks together had a long-term consequence. Each Saturday morning, the parents reviewed the previous week's behavior with the children. In all families that had previously used allowance as an incentive, the marks were assigned monetary values to match existing allowance rates. For example, in some families each G earned the child 10 cents (maximum week's total, $1.40), and each unacceptable behavior subtracted 5 cents from the total. In all cases the week's minimum was set at zero rather than having a child incur a debt for a particularly bad week. One family had not previously used monetary incentives, but had instead used family outings; for example, bowling on Saturday afternoons had been withheld when the child had misbehaved. In this family, we systematized the delivery of various types of family outings in a manner similar to that used for money in other families.

Physical Punishment

We superimposed on this system a second system of rewards and punishments. Since all of these families had typically used physical punishments in the form of apparently minor and nonphysically damaging spanks, and all but one had used rewards in the form of money or allowance, these features were incorporated into the system. Whether these families are normal might be debated; however, recent surveys show that use of some form of physical punishment in the family setting is the rule rather than the exception (Miller, 1984, page 58). In subsequent applications with other families, we have tailored the rewards and punishments to the incentives already being used in the family; many families do not employ spanking, and most of those that do have eventually been able to omit this feature.

In all families I have worked with, I have worked to eliminate physical punishment.[1] I learned very early that it would do no good to preach to parents about right and wrong ways to raise children or about how to use rewards and punishments. In fact, it seemed as if such preaching could do harm: some of the families I worked with early in my career got upset over what they saw as preaching and left treatment. I also learned that many parents believe in the proverb "sparing the rod will spoil the child". This belief simply would not yield to my direct argument. Accordingly, I developed several strategies to help lessen the severity, duration, and frequency of spankings, as well as to help parents resist sudden angry impulses to hit. The simplest strategy was to contract with the parent to hit him- or herself on the thigh at least three times before hitting the child – in the same manner and as hard as the child was to be hit. This had at least two effects: (1) Parents realized what damage and pain might be inflicted, and (2) The severity and duration of hitting was usually lessened (and sometimes the parent refrained from hitting the child at all).

I have also used a more complex method of working toward total omission of physical punishment. In those families that insisted on continuing to spank "when necessary," we agreed that a spank would be administered only when a child had indulged in three consecutive incidents within the same category of unacceptable behavior, or in five incidents across categories. The spank was administered immediately after the final mark was obtained (three or five); as mentioned above, the chart entries were made when each incident of unacceptable behavior occurred. I stressed to the parents that the child should be told of the mark being put on the chart and that this announcement (or the spank when necessary) should as a rule signal the end of the attention gained by the child for the unacceptable behavior. In cases where a child continued to be dangerous, destructive, or intensely disruptive he or she was removed, isolated, and ignored for a "time-out" period of five minutes. This additional step was rarely necessary, since the entry of a mark on the chart generally ended such behavior.

---

[1] I was occasionally spanked as a child, and I confess that I spanked each of my four children at least once; I also should note that my wife and I used a form of the program described here to help us avoid such behavior.

Each spank was denoted on the chart with an asterisk.   After a spank, the child started anew, in the sense that the next single unacceptable behavior was the beginning of a new series.   Children also started with a clean slate each morning, in that no marks for unacceptable behavior from the previous day were counted toward a spank on the subsequent day.

Some Data

Table 5.3 shows some of the data from these five normal families. In all cases daily occurrences of physical punishment were monitored by the parents for a four-week baseline period prior to the onset of the program, and the table compares this baseline with the frequency of physical punishment during the program.   On this index, the program   resulted in a clear improvement, with the frequency of physical punishment at the end approaching zero in all five families.   In the three families (numbers 2, 4, and 5) for which we have informal, longer-term follow-up, the frequencies of physical punishment have for 12 more months remained at or below the levels shown in Table 5.3.   Other indications of a more desirable level of function in all five families varied from family to family. One of the most notable changes was the realization that each child thrived on undivided attention from a single parent (i.e., one-to-one interaction).   Each family devised some format for indefinitely maintaining this feature, and this outlasted the formal monitoring of behavior and programming of incentives.

Table 5.3
Some Effects of the Use of Behavior-Control Technique in Five Normal Families

Family	Number of boys (ages)	Number of girls (ages)	Mean Weekly Number of Physical Punishments per Child During:			Mean Weekly Number for the Most Recent Month of:		Total duration of chart use	Modification to chart procedure described in text
			the month before the start of chart use	the last week of the second month of chart use	the most recent month of chart use	Bad marks	Good marks		
1	2 (9,8)	1 (5)	2	1	.1	6	7	31 mo.	Maximum number of G = 1 per day.
2	2 (10,7)	1 (4)	2	0	.1	6	7	10 mo.	maximum number of G = 1 per day.
3	1 (5 1/2)		7	1	.25	6	14	8 mo.	G is given at the time of occurrence of certain target behaviors (maximum of 5 G's per day) if child gets more G's than bad marks he earns a family outing (e.g., bowling).
4	1 (8)	1 (6)	4	1	.5	10	9	4 mo.	G = 5 cents, bad marks = 2 cents
5	2 (4 1/2) Twins	1 (5 1/2)	21	0	.25	10	9	4mo.	Chart is discussed in evening befoire prayers; G = 5 cents, bad marks = 1 cents

Application With Troubled Families

We have also applied the program with dozens of families that would not be considered normal. I will present three such families as illustrations. The second and third of these families were clinically judged to be abusive.

A Boy With Problems

One troubled – but not clinically abusive – family came to us complaining about the behavioral problems of their seven-year-old boy. This boy was the older of two children, residing with his family in a suburban middle-class home. He was doing average work in school, although his intelligence was superior. His behavior in the home showed long periods of normal behavior, with daily shorter periods of intensely disruptive behavior (see Figure 5.1). His disruptive behavior included the following: severe tantrums in which he would destroy furniture, draperies, and belongings; incidents of apparently unprovoked verbal and physical abuse (some of which was very dangerous) toward his younger sister; and incidents of making very loud noises and creating various disturbances when others preferred quiet (in church and in the middle of the night). The parents had tried to deal with him in various ways before bringing him to us with their tearful plea for help.

Conversation with the parents and child suggested the following:

(1) The child's self-esteem was low or "Not OK" as reflected in word counts, in good and bad categories, and in response to the request "tell me about yourself."
(2) The child felt guilty about his behavior.
(3) The parents confessed that they had frequently resorted to spankings (apparently more severe than those used in the families described in the preceding section) and to guilt-producing statements in an attempt to control the child's behavior.
(4) Reports from both the parents and the child on what happened before and after his misbehaviors indicated that he was reinforced by parental attention and that he very rarely received parental attention that was not contingent on bad behavior.

Figure 5.1. *Disruptive behavior of a seven-year-old boy over a 16-week period.*

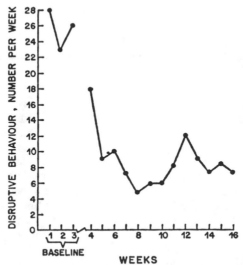

We implemented the program and some of the results are shown in Figure 5.1. The parents reported that the disruptive behaviors occurring after approximately the sixth week were much less prolonged and less disturbing to the other members of the family. A follow-up evaluation 15 months after instituting the program showed that the boy's frequency of disruptive behavior remained at the level shown in the final four weeks covered in Figure 5.1. However, his parents reported that certain disruptive behaviors no longer occurred (such as tantrums involving destruction of furniture and his sister's belongings and physical abuse of his sister) and that the remaining disruptive behaviors were relatively mild and brief.

According to the parents' reports, this boy's behavior outside of the home and with his schoolmates, while not a target problem, was improved markedly after the institution of the program. This suggests that his new style of behavior became generalized since his new style showed even without a targeted and programmed scheme of rewards and punishments. His school grades also improved.

Finally, his self-esteem, as reflected by self-references, shifted to the point where bad references were hardly ever present and where neutral and good references predominated (a standardized self-esteem measure for children was not used here).

Abusive Parents

The program has also been used with numerous abusive parents. Often these family settings are highly disorganized, and we always involve the appropriate civil authorities.[2]

In one abusive family, the average number of episodes of hitting per child (there were three boys, aged three to seven) was about 19 per week during the baseline period.[3] One of the boys was brain-damaged, and this may have resulted from hitting. The parents admitted that some of their previous hits had been closed-fist assaults above the neck. By the time the program had been in effect for six weeks, the frequency of physical intervention had dropped to one per week per child, and the severity had decreased to a far less dangerous level (according to reports from both parents). The family stayed on the program for at least five years, and we received periodic reports over the five-year period indicating that the lower frequency and severity had been stabilized. No further damage to any of the children could be detected by our evaluation (see Figure 5.2).

In a second abusive family (two girls, aged two and five, and one boy, aged three and a half), the mother was hitting the oldest daughter from 6 to 16 times per week during the baseline period. By the time the program had been in effect for six weeks, the average frequency of physical intervention had dropped to less than one hit per week, and again, according to the mother, the severity of these interventions was reduced to a far less dangerous level (see Figure 5.3).

[2] Great caution must be exercised in all aspects of dealing with cases of abuse. Civil authorities, such as state social service department employees, generally seem well equipped – with an understanding of legal options, and with training to make a correct clinical judgment about the degree of danger to the child.

[3] Baseline periods when abuse is confessed, are usually retrospective estimates. However, in this case I did not know that abuse was occurring until after the last baseline week. In this family both parents made separate counts that corresponded well; also, the oldest boy corroborated the counts given by his parents.

Figure 5.2. *Median (range shown in brackets) number of physical interventions (father or mother to three sons) over a 34-week period.*

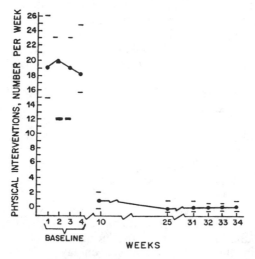

Figure 5.3. *Physical interventions (mother to five-year-old daughter) over a 12-week period.*

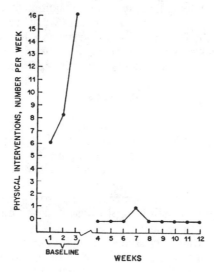

Both of these abusive families (and all other abusive families I've seen) required long-term family therapy. The adults and the children received various forms of individual counseling and therapy. These services were provided by other caregivers who occasionally consulted with me.

Summary

From the information I have gathered, I am left with the following impressions:

(1)   The abusive families profited from the long-term use of the optimization program
(2)   The families needed frequent reminding and prodding to maintain systematic use of the program
(3)   The families had greatest difficulty in
      [a] making proper use of the program when they suddenly became upset and had the urge to hit and in
      [b] scheduling and giving noncontingent (or clock-contingent) positive attention each day
(4)   The families and the individual members had many problems that required long-term attention from well-trained, talented, creative and tenacious caregivers
(5)   The most successful caregivers were those who maintained the optimization program as a low-cost and humane background condition, and who went on to attend to remaining problems using other methods.

Advantages

In the families described in this chapter, in all but the final case the basic method of assessment was the entry of letters on the chart. In the first abusive family, where each parent was abusive, the parents reported separately on each other's behavior. In the final case, the family with the single abusive parent, two methods of record keeping were used, which permitted a cross-check. All data demonstrated a rapid reduction in physical punishment soon after implementation of the program.

As mentioned earlier, we have some evidence that the program effect outlasts its formal application. One of the normal families (the second shown in Table 5.1) was periodically observed before, during, and after the use of the program. These observations suggest that the behavior patterns developed in all family members during use of the program (for 11 months) continued for more than 10 years after its termination. For example, while the mean weekly average of physical punishments per child prior to the program was two, no physical punishments occurred during the post-program observation period.

A very important aspect of the program was control of parental behavior beyond the demonstrated reduction in use of physical punishment. For example, systematizing and ensuring the parental attention given to the disruptive seven-year-old boy may well have been the basis for the change found in that case. In many less-troubled families we have observed significant positive change as a result only of ensuring the daily period of parental attention (with no control over other behaviors or incentives). In the abusive families, uncoupling the parental mood swings from the parental behavioral outbursts was an important result of the use of this program. The most important force in this uncoupling may have been the prescription of a specific parental response to a child's misbehavior.

We also have some evidence that the program effects generalize to other settings and to changes in behaviors outside the home (such as the dramatic improvement in school behavior and in grades shown by the seven-year-old boy).

Turning to consideration of self-esteem, or self-concept, and sense of agency, we also have some evidence. For example, in addition to the improvement in one child's self-esteem in the second abusive family, the mother reported that she also experienced dramatic improvement in her self-concept and her sense of self-control during the use of the program. In some subsequent applications, we did a careful assessment of the self-concept of all members of the families being treated, and we occasionally assessed other dependent variables (such as contracting skills). All subsequently gathered data supported the observations described above.

This program differs markedly from the most popular format in which Skinner's plan has been applied. The most important difference is that we match the reinforcement schedules and contingencies to those that apparently prevail in the real world.[4]

The objective of matching, sequencing, or programming

---

[4] This program also answers some of Skinner's complaints about punishment in that it (1) depersonalizes punishment and (2) makes punishment events "informationally strong."

generalization has received attention from workers concerned with therapeutic applications of programs based on Skinner's plan. Numcrous reviews of progress in this area (e.g., Kazdin and Bootzin, 1972) suggest the need for continuing work on this problem. Furthermore, in a non-clinical application, Feallock and Miller (1976) examined the high failure rate of experimental group living arrangements that were based on Skinner's ideas. The data they present demonstrate that the living arrangements become more stable when both negative and positive incentives are included and when contingencies more closely approximate those prevailing in the real world.

In addition to the advantages already cited, the family optimization program may have the following added values:

(1) Low cost in time required for administration
(2) A team approach to negotiating contracts
(3) A "boilerplate" strategy that implies the expectation of good behavior and removes the necessity of rewarding each episode of good behavior
(4) The control of parental attention which in some cases is very difficult to manage properly, and which in many cases can provide the solution to many problems.

6 : Troubled Families With Preverbal Children

Procedures for preventing the abuse of preverbal children have received little attention in the literature. Procedures that have been documented are generally more appropriate for families whose children are verbal and are over one year old.

In one published report, Sanders (1978) described the use of systematic desensitization with an infant-abusing parent. This effective treatment stemmed from Sanders's observation:

> An infant's crying can cause the parent to become anxious and frustrated, and this in turn may lead to an episode of abuse.

His observation is supported by data on the physiological and emotional effects of an infant's crying on adults (Frodi and Lamb, 1980). Our experiences with many anxious couples who had preverbal children, and with three parents who severely abused their infants, further support Saunders's observation.

In fact, some parents report feeling that the crying infant is intentionally tormenting them (supported by data of Bauer and Twentyman, 1985). The interaction thus becomes an unequal power struggle. Parents have also confessed to me that they feel the presence of a judgmental entity (a "critic function") in the infant, or in their own minds; the infant's crying translates into an accusation that the parent is a bad parent or a failure.

Many children spend a lot of time crying, and even the very young infant will fuss or cry for parental attention. Crying usually does lead to either positive or neutral parental attention, but it can also lead to negative parental attention. The parent's negative attention may begin and end with a minor physical intervention such as a pat on the fanny. With an abusing parent, though, the negative attention often escalates rapidly to a level at which tissue damage occurs (an abusive episode).

Christopherson and colleagues (1976) have emphasized the value of using time-out procedures in conjunction with written protocols in order to help parents avoid using corporal punishment. We have combined these methods in a specific format for coping with the fussing of preverbal infants. This format addresses two fundamental objectives by (1) breaking the connection between the infant's fussing and the negative parental attention, while (2) guiding and supporting the parents as they learn to give positive attention when the infant is not fussing.

The Time-Out Procedure

For breaking the connection between fussing and negative attention, we have successfully used a simple behavioral procedure revolving around a time-out technique. The procedure involves a checking routine, a time-out period, record keeping, instructions on positive attention (all presented in Table 6.1), and therapist support. A key element in the procedure is for the parent to leave the child shortly after the start of an episode of fussing and after a routine check for problems. In about half of the cases we have seen, the infant initially showed an increase in the intensity, duration, or frequency of crying.[1] Since this increase in crying may last from three to seven days, the therapist should try to make frequent supportive contacts by phone or in person, at least every third day, with one or both of the parents. In the ideal circumstance these contacts should continue at a frequency of twice a week for at least two weeks and can then be phased out gradually over the next two to four weeks. (You will see, in Tables 6.2 and 6.3, that I have not been very successful in combining support with data gathering.) Support helps the parents (and the infants) to persist long enough to realize the benefits of the strategy. This also seems necessary to help parents take seriously and abide by the instructions for giving daily positive attention.

[1] Drabman and Jarvie, working with older, verbal children also noted an increase in misbehavior and crying in the early stages of using a time-out procedure (Pediatrics, 1977, 59, pages 78-85).

Table 6.1
Time-Out Procedure for Baby's Crying Episodes

INSTRUCTIONS
When baby starts crying: 1) write down time; 2) go through prescribed routine and enter finishing time below; 3) wait 30 minutes (if possible go for a walk, or somehow occupy your- self); 4) if baby is still crying, repeat first three steps.

Date	Time when crying started	Time when you finish the "check" routine? (Check diapers, pins, sheets, blankets, gas, and for possible hunger.)	After finishing the "check" routine, what did you do in the 30 minute waiting period?	Was baby crying at end of the 30 min.? (If so, repeat "check" routine and 30 minute cycle. Record this new cycle as a new episode on this page.)

Remember: A) During "check" routine, do not yell or show any emotion. Make it as mechanical as possible. B) Give the baby attention when he/she is not crying; schedule at least half an hour in the morning and half an hour in the evening to play with the baby; this will help the baby learn to cry only when he/she is in need of help.

Table 6.2

Crying and Abuse of Preverbal Children

Family	Measure	Preprogram Week	During program Week1	During program Week 2	Follow-up Duration
1 (Mr. D)	Number of cries	20	17 [0,5,3,1,5,2,1]	8 [0,3,1,1,1,1]	10 Years
	Duration of cries	(30 min.)	(5 min.)	(5 min.)	
	Number of physical interventions	14	0	0	
2 (Mrs. S)	Number of cries	(100+)	(35) [12,7](5 estimates of less than 5)	23 [4,1,0,6,4,7,1]	1 1/2 Years
	Duration of cries	(5 min.)	(5 Min. +)	(2 min. ±)	
	Number of physical interventions	(1-2)	0	0	
3 (Dr. G)	Number of cries	(14)	(35) [5](6 estimates of 5)	22 [3,2,6,2,3,4,2]	2 Years
	Duration of cries	(60 min.)	(10 min. +)	(10 min. ±)	
	Number of physical interventions	(5)	0	0	

Note: Estimates are in parentheses. Daily numbers from charts are in brackets. In Family 3, Dr. G's mother was present for the first program week. In Family 1 the subsequent frequency of physical intervention varies--see text.

Table 6.3
Crying of Preverbal Children

Family	Measure	Preprogram Week 1	Week 2
4	Number of Cries	(24 times per day)	(24 times per day)
	Duration	(15 minutes)	(15 minutes)
5	Number of Cries	(28 times per day)	(28 times per day)
	Duration	(1 to 30 minutes)	(1 to 30 minutes)
6	Number of Cries	(7 to 10 times per day)	(7 to 10 times per day)
	Duration	(15 minutes +)	(15 minutes)
7	Number of Cries	[7 (6 estimates of 5 + times)]	[(5 estimates of 5+ times) 2,6]
	Duration	(20 minutes)	(20 minutes)
8	Number of Cries	(7 estimates of 2 times)	[1,3,2,0,2,1,1]
	Duration	(1 hour each time)	(fluctuating-range 5hrs to 2hrs)
9	Number of Cries	(7 estimates of 2 times per night)	(2 times per night)
	Duration	(15+ minutes)	(15 minutes each time)
10	Number of Cries	(7 estimates of at least 1)	(7 estimates of 1 time per night)
	Duration	(30 minutes)	(30 minutes)
11	Number of Cries	(7 estimates of 1 or 2)	[(6 estimates of 1 or 2) 1]
	Duration	(at least 30 minutes)	(30 minutes)
12	Number of Cries	(7 estimates of 3 to 5)	[(6 estimates of 3 to 5) 4]
	Duration	(at least 15 minutes)	(15 minutes each)

Note: Estimates are in parentheses. Daily numbers from charts are in brackets.

Table 6.3 (continued)

Family	During Program	
	Week 1	Week 2
4	[15,10,18,12,7,(7),10] (15 minutes +)	[(10) (20) 10, 17, 4, 7, 5] (10 minutes)
5	[10] (6 estimates of "more than 10") (15 minutes)	(7 estimates of 5 times per day) (25 minutes)
6	[6 (16)(12)(12) 9,15 (5)] (15 to 30 minutes)	[(4 estimates of 5) 5, (3), 3] (15 minutes +)
7	[2, 0, 1, 3, 2, 1, 1] (30 to 60 minutes)	[(6 estimates 1-2 times) 2] (less than 10 minutes)
8	[2 (2) 3, 3, 3, 0, 1] (decreasing from 1 hour to 5 minutes)	(7 estimates of 0-2 times) (none more than 15 minutes)
9	[3, 1, 2, (2) 0, 1, 0] (30 minutes each time)	("He sleeps through most nights, maybe outgrew it".)
10	[1 (3), 2] (4 estimates of 1 each night) (10-20 minutes)	[1,2, (1), 1, 3, (3), 1] (5 minutes)
11	(7 estimates of 1) (more than 30 minutes for 1 or 2 nights then less)	[(6 estimates of 1) 1] (less than 2 minutes)
12	[2, 5, 1, 2, 1, 0, 1] (fluctuating-range 15 minutes to 1.5 hours)	[0, 2, 3, 2, 0, 1, 1] (15 to 5 minutes)

Table 6.3 (continued)

Family	Follow-up Duration	Comments
4	None	Both parents are nurses; work different shifts.
5	3 months	Single parent & sitter did estimates; child cried 1 time in the day before last follow-up visit, 15 minutes.
6	2 years	Physician husband, nurse wife, & sitter did counting.
7	None	Parents and several sitters did counting.
8	None	Counted only cries at night.
9	None	Counted only cries at night.
10	1 Month	Counted only cries at night; follow-up at 1 month-"He cries 1 time most nights-but only for a couple of minutes."
11	10 Days	Counted only cries at night.
12	6 Months	Counted only cries at night; 6 month follow-up "1 cry for 5 minutes or less."

As mentioned above, we have used the procedure with three infant-abusing parents (see Table 6.2) and with many couples who did not report abusing their infants but who reported feeling extremely anxious when their infants cried (data for nine families are presented in Table 6.3). The following paragraphs illustrate the use of this procedure with a particularly troubled abusive parent (Mr. D reappears later, especially in Chapter 13).

Mr. D

Mr. D was a 27-year-old Vietnam veteran who was married and unemployed. He had a high-school education. Initially, Mr. D was referred to the Psychology Section at the White River Junction, Vermont, Veterans Hospital for treatment of serious generalized anxiety. A detailed psychological and neurological assessment indicated that Mr. D had some organic impairment resulting from a head injury, was experiencing difficulty with impulse control, was mildly depressed, and was fearful of social situations. During the assessment phase, Mr. D assured us that his family life, with his wife and his preverbal 11-month-old stepdaughter, was not a source of difficulty.

Following the psychological assessment, we conducted four sessions of progressive-relaxation training with Mr. D over a 10-day period. At the last of these sessions, Mr. D reported that he was feeling much less anxious and depressed. He then mentioned, for the first time, that he was having a persistent problem with disciplining his stepdaughter. He would become very angry with her. As he said, "She cries all the time, and I think she knows what it does to us." Although Mr. D admitted to spanking his stepdaughter, he did not at the time mention using excessive force. Nonetheless, considering the client's own obvious concern, we decided to attend to this issue.

Mr. D agreed to record the time of each incident of anger toward his stepdaughter, what caused him to become angry, and what he did about it. At the end of the first week, Mr. D's record showed that he had become angry with the child 20 times (each time she cried) and that he had hit her 14 times. Discussion revealed that some of these blows were severe enough to cause physical injury, and that such episodes had been occurring since the child was about 5 months old. Our subsequent conversations with the mother corroborated Mr. D's statements, and examination of the daughter revealed multiple bruises and scars. (At this time Mr. D also revealed that he had been abused as a child and that he was ashamed that he was doing "the same thing" to his child.)

We then instituted the time-out procedure. (State social services were also notified,[2] and they made weekly visits for several months and occasional visits over the next six years.) Mr. D was given a page of instructions, along with a record-keeping format (see Table 6.1). This page was taped to the wall of the child's room. Mr. D and his wife were instructed to use the format and to keep a record of what happened whenever a crying episode occurred. Mr. D was instructed to bring the completed record for the week to each session.

After using this procedure for two weeks, Mr. D had reduced his frequency of hitting the child to zero, and the frequency of the child's crying had gone from more than two episodes per day in the first week to about one per day in the second week. During an initial 18-month follow-up period for this problem[3], we had ten meetings, most of which involved a discussion with both parents and an examination of the child. These sessions also involved systematic desensitization and biofeedback for control of autonomic arousal and cognitive treatments for anger. We found no evidence of further physical abuse that extended to causing tissue damage. However, Mr. D and his wife did occasionally resort to physical interventions. They classified these interventions as "normal spankings" or "pats on the fanny." The state social service personnel and I had many discussions with Mr. and Mrs. D about this issue. The repeated debates over "spare the rod and spoil the child" seemed to get us nowhere. However, this program was used with fair consistency by Mr. and Mrs. D for five years and four months. They also apparently abided by my rule regarding hitting their own thigh before hitting the child (see Chapter 5). However, they were not able to consistently incorporate other components of the mutual control strategy described in Chapter 5. The data and our own experiences with physical intervention in the D family are summarized in the following paragraphs.

---

[2] Again, great caution must be exercised in all aspects of dealing with cases of abuse; state social service employees have training which improves their chances of making a correct judgment about the degree of danger to a child.

[3] We later saw Mr. D for problems with violent behavior toward other adults; details of this treatment are presented in subsequent chapters.

The last detected tissue damage was that detected immediately prior to onset of the program. The only known episodes that appeared to be outside of the "pat on the fanny" range occurred in a four-day period five weeks after the start of the program – these did not result in detectable tissue damage and the social service representative decided to leave the child in the home. The number of spankings each week was four or less for the first year, and two or less for the next four years. In the five years after termination of the formal program, there were no occasions on which physical intervention occurred more than once per week.

Throughout the follow-up period, Mr. D maintained most of the gains he had realized in the first four sessions of progressive relaxation. He showed better impulse control and a steady decrease in his fear of social situations. He also reported an increase in his ability to prevent and control feelings of anger and a decrease in the anxiety and frustration he felt when his stepdaughter cried.

Advantages

This procedure has proven effective both in reducing an infant's crying and in stopping abuse of the infant. Used alongside the program described in Chapter 5, this procedure has helped to stabilize several large and highly disorganized families with two or more children ranging from infancy to late adolescence. It has also been used successfully with families of various socioeconomic levels. Mr. D's family was the least well educated and the most disadvantaged of our small clinical sample of three families who abused preverbal infants. In the other two infant-abusing families, the parents were both college educated and one was a practicing physician.

The procedure is quite simply applied using the framework and instructions in Table 6.1. As the use of this procedure dissociates parental attention from behavioral episodes that elicit negative attention, it not only decreases the likelihood of abuse, but it also lays the foundation for a positive parent-child relationship. With less pressure for the child to misbehave in order to get attention, the child is free to learn new ways of getting attention, and the parent can practice new ways of giving it. In all of the families treated, use of the routine has increased the frequency of positive interaction and has apparently aided in the formation of a positive relationship between parent and child.

Beyond the advantage of its apparently wide applicability, the procedure has two significant technical advantages. First, the procedure is easy to teach and learn and thus can be instituted rapidly. Second, the parents' use of the system can be easily monitored. Both of these features are of obvious importance when we are intervening in so serious a problem as infant abuse.

The procedure and our system for its use can also have certain operational efficiencies. The probability of negative parental attention is decreased as the parent follows a prescribed routine that specifies both an appropriate direct response to the infant's crying (the neutral checking routine) and a method for coping with negative reactions (the 30-minute waiting or time-out routine). The parent is thus separated from the infant during the period when abuse is most likely to occur. Positive episodes of parental attention are programmed, and these episodes are clearly separated from the infant's crying behavior.

Positive parental attention has not been carefully programmed in many published procedures for dealing with abuse. Parents often need to be reminded regularly of this aspect of the program in order for them to take it seriously. Many parents act as if it were best to leave the infant alone when he or she is quiet. Doing so they put the infant in a bind; specifically, the infant is addicted to attention and if enough is not given he or she will be forced to work for it – that is, to cry. Those published procedures (e.g., Drabman and Jarvie, 1977) that do attend to the management of positive attention generally try to arrange for it to be contingent upon positive behavior of the child. While the child should frequently be rewarded for good behavior, it is also crucially important that the child not be forced to "earn" all positive attention. As emphasized earlier, it is the non-behavior- contingent (or clock-contingent) positive attention from the parents that will help develop the self-concept in the child that he or she is loved. One who must get attention by doing tricks – or "polishing apples" – does not necessarily develop the good self-concept.

Sanders (1978) combined systematic desensitization with various other procedures, including medication, counseling, and supportive psychotherapy. His program took more than 13 months, including 12 sessions of systematic desensitization, and it required considerable cooperation from the patient. It is worth noting that, in our sample, Mr. D was the only client for whom we used systematic desensitization, biofeedback, or anger-management training. Many abusing parents do of course require long-term treatment. In the meantime, our time-out procedure can be instituted at the first or second visit so that risk of further abuse can be reduced while the other parts of the intervention (including the involvement of appropriate social services) get underway.

7 : Troubled Adults

Having considered some ideas and methods pertaining to families and the development of individual personalities, let's reconsider what happens when things go wrong. One thing at least should be obvious by now: I believe that most behavioral problems can be traced to problems in the impact of incentives, and, in turn, to self-concept. I also believe that many behavioral problems can be traced all the way back to the management by parents of their attention to their children.

Mismanaged Parental Attention

The power and effect of mismanagement of parental attention can be illustrated in various ways. One of the most frequent problems arises when the child learns that misbehavior is the only reliable method of getting desired parental attention. Misbehaving in order to get attention usually has several effects, of which the following five are quite frequent:

(1) Misbehavior usually results in further fogging of the boundaries between positive and negative attention, or between the intended positive affective messages and the intended negative affective messages from the parent.

(2) This fogging usually causes both the child and the parent to expect misbehavior.

(3) Once they expect misbehavior, the parents are less likely to spontaneously give attention to the child, and they may even begin to avoid the child.

(4) The child will begin to perceive the essential audience, or significant others, as having a negative and critical attitude toward him or her (see Figure 4.8 in Chapter 4).
(5) The child's general self-concept develops in the "I am not OK" direction (see Figure 4.7 and 4.10 in Chapter 4).

Thus, the child who learns to misbehave in order to get attention will eventually come to feel "not OK," will have difficulty differentiating intended positive social incentives from negative social incentives, and may well develop unusual responses to other forms of incentives if this pattern continues.

Some evidence supports the notion that a reversal in the impact of incentives can develop. This reversal may be associated with environmental factors in addition to the fogging that can occur in early learning. J. McV. Hunt (1972) examined the relationship between self-esteem and preferred incentives, with socioeconomic level as a related variable. Children at lower socioeconomic levels, who show lowered self-esteem (Coleman, 1966; Keller, 1963; Long and Henderson, 1967), show greater preference for concrete rewards such as M&M candies than they do for symbolic incentives such as praise or knowledge of results (Terrel, Durkin, and Weisley, 1959; Zigler and DeLabry, 1962). Children at lower socioeconomic levels also tend to prefer immediate delivery of incentives over delayed delivery of incentives, even when the incentive to be obtained later would be greater. On the other hand, children of higher socioeconomic levels prefer to wait for the larger, but delayed, incentive (Maitland, 1966; Mischel, 1961; Mischel and Metzner, 1962; Steen, 1966).

In depressed adults (who generally show lower self-esteem) investigators (Lewinsohn, Weinstein, and Shaw, 1969; Miller and Seligman, 1976) have observed alterations in incentive responsiveness. Rehm and Plakosh (1975) demonstrated that the higher a person's depression score (measured by a multiple- adjective checklist), the greater would be the person's preference for immediate delivery of incentive.

Incentive Stimuli Inverted

Taken together, these ideas and data might lead one to believe that a complete inversion, or reversal, of the impact of an incentive stimulus could take place in certain circumstances. In fact, as I think about some of the depressed adults and adults with low self-esteem whom I have known, I quickly recall examples of apparent reversal of the impact of intended positive social incentives. There are various mechanisms by which this might happen. Consider the following five possibilities:

(1) *An intended positive incentive may carry a conditioned negative component.* For example, a child who is repeatedly told, "That's nice, but why can't you do it every time?" may experience both positive and negative incentives. The child may hear, "The behavior is nice, but you are not expected to show that nice behavior on a regular basis." It seems that the repeated experiencing of such communications could fit the classical conditioning model such that the receiver experiences a negative incentive, even when the message seems totally positive to the sender.

(2) *The occurrence of a positive incentive may sharpen the expectancy of a negative incentive.* This may happen because the individual is functioning as if he or she were on a schedule for incentive delivery.

(3) *A positive incentive may signal "time out" from future positive incentives.* Again, this may happen because the individual is functioning as if he or she were on a schedule for incentive delivery(e.g., low ratio). The comment, "Well, that's my good luck for today," seems to fit this model.

(4) *The delivery of an intended positive incentive may increase or sharpen feelings of unworthiness or guilt* (see Figure 4.9 in Chapter 4). This is a dynamic explanation of a phenomenon epitomized by the person who is unable to accept a compliment. For example, if one attempts to compliment such a person on a painting, he or she might say, "Well, thank you, but that was just a lucky one, and really not much good; if you look closely, you'll see that the good effect is produced by the cat getting into my paint and dragging its tail across the picture." Some such people actually seem afraid to enjoy compliments. Perhaps they fear that the omnipresent essential audience will criticize them for rejoicing in their own accomplishments.

(5) *The occurrence of a positive incentive may be seen as a random event, or as an event that was not produced or controlled by the individual.* Even though the individual may show some signs of pleasure at the occurrence of the positive incentive, he or she may experience an increase in the sense of helplessness, or even in the sense that he or she is being controlled by someone else. Thus the positive incentive can again be seen as having a negative component.

A large body of research by Seligman and his colleagues provides support for such notions (e.g., Miller and Seligman, 1976).

Tracing Back

Such mechanisms and examples of the relationship between incentives, depression, and self-esteem can be taken to great lengths. They can sometimes be clarified in an individual so that a specific behavioral problem will be traceable to problems in incentive impact, and in turn to self-concept, and finally all the way back to delivery of attention by parents.

One of the best-known examples of tracing an adult behavioral problem back to the parents' strategies of managing their attention is that of the paranoid German man described by Schatzman (1973) in a book appropriately entitled, *Soul Murder.* The man's father had developed and published a general program for raising children and had described his tactics in great detail. The concepts of the essential audience and the critic function are starkly illustrated by Schatzman's quotes from the man's writing, and the writing shows how a disapproving glance can eventually come to have a very large effect on a child's behavior.

Goleman (1985) considered the same case and juxtaposed with it the consideration of some children who were in therapy because they had been abused by their parents. These latter children also showed features of paranoia and the critic function in their self-labelling behavior (e.g., "bad," "stupid"), and in other areas of their behavior as well. Goleman says,

> In these tragic children denial and displacement – key mechanisms of the paranoid style – are already in place. These paranoid predispositions need not come

from such explosive events as abuse; these same
tendencies can be imprinted on the mind by less
obvious forms of tyranny. Violence can come in
subtler forms – as disapproving looks, silent rebuffs,
humiliation, or love withdrawn. The net effect can
be the same, provided the implicit injunction is
instilled: that the parent is blameless for the feelings
of hurt and anger that the child feels   (page 153).

The critic function established by the parents can lead to criticism
of both self and others and to related expectancies and dispositions
that become involved in a reciprocally determined tangle of
relationships between the working self-concept and the behavior of
other people.

A child who expects rejection from his parents may
become hyper-alert to signs of it in his playmates.
Such a child is likely   to distort innocuous
comments, seeing them as hostile. In anticipation of
such hostility, a child prepares to counter it by
meeting his playmates with a cold, rigid stare and
some aggressive words. This in turn evokes the
very response it was meant to anticipate – the child
becomes the target of his playmates' real rather than
imagined hostility (Goleman, 1985, page 153).

Goleman has thus provided an excellent description of what
appears to be going on in the interactions of my violent clients with
other people, including what goes on with their own infants.

Part Three

Technique

8 : Assessment Approaches

In our attempts to understand the tangled processes I have described, my colleagues and I have used a wide variety of assessment procedures and mini-modeling strategies.

Some Options

For the exploration of incentive responsiveness, we have used behavioral interviews and procedures such as behavioral-avoidance tests, roleplaying, and naturalistic observation. We have assessed self-concepts using various formats for self-description (such as that used in the Dartmouth Pain Questionnaire, Corson and Schneider, 1984), and we have observed self-labeling behavior and expectancies and explanations of outcome in response to several behavioral assessment procedures. We have also used the following: (1) asking clients to underline words that describe themselves from a long list of possible self-labels; (2) asking clients to write descriptions of themselves that might be written by their best friend, their worst enemy, and by themselves; and (3) asking clients to keep records on their best and worst social experiences each day.

A combination of techniques generally gives us some idea of the development and status of our clients' self-concepts and of various important social incentives. Over the years, though, we have come to favor a simple four-part query, and for the past several years we have been using it with every client on almost every visit. This technique (briefly mentioned in Chapter 1) consists of asking the client four questions about self-satisfaction:

(1) What has been your highest level of self-satisfaction in the past 24 hours (on a 0-to-5 scale, where 0 is no satisfaction, 1 is just noticeable, and 5 is as high a level as is realistically possible, given the constraints of your life)?
(2) What was happening, or what were you doing, when you felt this high level of self-satisfaction?
(3) What has been your lowest level of self-satisfaction in the past 24 hours (on the same scale)?
(4) What was happening, or what were you doing, when you felt this low level of self-satisfaction?

The ABC Chart

Chapter 9 goes into detail on the format and mini-modeling routines we use in the attempt to relate incentive events to self-concept and behavior. The results of mini-modeling for four clients are presented now to illustrate some of the complexity we face in dealing with individual clients. Figures 8.1 and 8.2 depict differences among individuals who were referred for the same behavioral problems. Figure 8.1 shows the ABC chart (for Antecedents, Behaviors, and Consequences) for two people with bulimia (persons who overeat and then induce vomiting). They showed marked differences in incentive responsiveness; for example, while the first client never vomited when alone, the second client (Ms. N, who is also depicted in figures in Chapter 9) made a serious suicide attempt when her vomiting was discovered. Figure 8.2 depicts antecedents, behaviors, and consequences for two exhibitionists who responded to very different incentive events. (The ABC chart itself was briefly introduced in Chapter 1; see Table 1.1 for a blank chart with instructions. Chapter 13 contains many more examples of uses of the ABC chart.)

The self-labeling or self-concept aspects reflected in these figures were most helpful clinically in specifying the details of important incentive events, as well as in specifying important subjective and objective antecedent events. In turn, the clarification of these issues was helpful in selecting appropriate assessment and treatment regimes.

Theoretical notions regarding the shifty personality and its important variables have led to methods for assessing and treating families and individuals, and the outcome data from these methods are encouraging. More specifically these theoretical notions have led to a general strategy for assessment and treatment, the features of which include:

(1) The strategy determines as much as possible about the client's self-concept and its relationships to those stimuli that the client responds to as stressors and incentives (attention and other social stimuli are particularly important).

(2) The strategy – used in conjunction with careful description of antecedents, behavior, and consequences – can help the therapist avoid the trap of noticing only those stimulus and response events that would have incentive value for him or her.

(3) The strategy can help the therapist and the client to develop appropriate mini-models to depict relationships between specific compelling situations and specific behaviors, and thus lay a foundation for advancing the therapeutic effort.

	Antecedents	Behaviors	Consequences (short term)
Client # 1 (Social)	Stressful social situation- in a conflict-has a request denied. (Working self-concept: NOT IN CONTROL NOT DOMINANT.)	Client eats a few bites of something (e.g., potato salad) and induces vomiting IN PRESENCE OF PERSON(S) TO BE CONTROLLED.	Pity -> Client gets her way. (Working self-concept: IN CONTROL, DOMINANT.)
Client # 2 (Alone, Ms. N)	Client has no date- is alone- feels lonely - frustrated. (Working self-concept: UNLOVED, GETTING FAT?, REJECTED AND GUILTY DUE TO PRIOR SEX EXPERIENCE, PRIOR OVEREATING.)	Client overeats and induces vomiting - ALONE.	Client relieved of full feeling from overeating. (Working self-concept: (1) FEELS LESS GUILTY PERHAPS BECAUSE SHE HAS NOW SUFFERED FOR HER SINS!; (2) KNOWS SHE WILL NOT GAIN WEIGHT FROM THE OVEREATING.)

Figure 8.1. *ABC diagrams for two bulimic clients.*

	Antecedents	Behaviors	Consequences (short term)
Client # 1 (confronting)	LONG TERM Social stress-e.g., client is humiliated by his boss (who is a female). (Working self-concept: LOWER SELF-ESTEEM, "NOT DOMINANT" "CONTROLLED.") SHORT TERM Woman isolated-where her screams will not bring immediate attention (Client sees her as a "victim").	Exposure of genitals (while facing woman, three to ten feet away, obstructing her escape route).	(IDEAL) Woman screams [orgasm not necessary] (working self-concept: Client FEELS HIGHER SELF-ESTEEM, "DOMINANT," "ASSERTIVE".)
Client # 2 (peripheral)	Woman in park or library (often where screams would bring immediate attention). (Working self-concept: UNNOTICED, UNLOVED, UNWANTED.)	Exposure of genitals (not in line of sight, usually in peripheral field, where woman might notice; 10 to 40 feet away, not obstructing an escape route).	(IDEAL) Woman does not scream (may notice but pretends to ignore client). Client masturbates to orgasm. (Working self-concept: CLIENT FEELS RELIEVED, A BIT ASHAMED, BUT FEELS THAT HE HAS "DONE SOMETHING" AND BEEN NOTICED.)

Figure 8.2. *ABC diagrams for two exhibitionists.*

9 : The Flow Diagram

The complexity shown in Figures 8.1 and 8.2 could easily become overwhelming if one did not have some sort of organizing format. I have developed such a format and call it the flow diagram. It provides me with a structure, and it forces me and my clients and colleagues to hypothesize about cause-effect relationships, to speculate about treatments that might follow our hypotheses, and to develop ways to evaluate these treatments. The diagram, or some aspects of the diagram, are almost always developed in close collaboration with the client.

Procedure

A blank flow diagram is shown in Figure 9.1. We start with the column marked Target Problems and list the various problems for which the client is seeking help. Next, we use the Stimuli column to list the important historical events and possible causes or triggers that might set off these target problems. Then the Presumed Internal Processes column is used to list the guesses or hypotheses regarding internal (psychodynamic?) variables that might link the Stimuli to the Target Problems. Following this, we use the Treatment Methods column to list and sequence the possible appropriate treatment procedures for each Target Problem. Finally, we use the Evaluation Methods column to specify procedures by which we will monitor the client's status and eventually measure the impact of treatment. The last column is crucial in the development of a personal scientist/theorist attitude. We must develop ways to assess the effects of our interventions in order to keep pace with the

Name _____ Education _____ Marital Status _____ Referred by _____

Date _____ Age _____ Occupation _____ Presenting Problems _____

STIMULI	PRESUMED INTERNAL PROCESSES	TARGET PROBLEMS	TREATMENT METHODS	EVALUATION METHODS

Figure 9.1. *Flow diagram format.*

inevitable shifts in the client's personality and in order to continue refining our theory and treatments.

Applications

Figure 9.2 shows an initial flow diagram for Ms. N, drawn after the first intake interview. (Ms. N was the second person with bulimia whose ABC chart appeared in Figure 8.1 .) Notice how quickly you get a feeling from the first two columns for the salient aspects that influence Ms. N's bulimia. Notice also that already some systematic evaluation is planned for the events surrounding her bulimia. You also see two other problems noted, but they are little understood after the first hour – Ms. N's apparent lack of social skills and her suicide attempt.

As treatment continues, the flow diagram is updated whenever new ideas or data can be added. As it always does, the picture gradually becomes more complex (Figure 9.3). We learned that Ms. N was severely troubled by complex developmental and psychodynamic issues. Most important was her relationship with a judgmental and controlling mother, with a resulting matrix of issues involving anger and control. Figure 9.3 depicts our hypotheses about the relationships among these psychodynamic issues and between these issues and other problems. Notice that even this more complex flow diagram gives an easy overview of the salient issues. Take, for example, the column entitled Treatment Methods. A team approach has evolved, with a therapist doing the behavioral work, coordinating it with an exercise coach, with those doing medical and dietary work, and with another therapist who treats intrapsychic problems.

Name F.N.   Education University Graduate   Marital Status Single   Referred by Dr. S. John

Date 3/4/74   Age 21   Occupation Social Work (internship)   Presenting Problems Self-induced

vomiting and stomach pain.

STIMULI	PRESUMED INTERNAL PROCESSES	TARGET PROBLEMS	TREATMENT METHODS	EVALUATION METHODS
Being alone	Self-concept: "unattractive, fat, guilty, angry, depressed"	Overeat (feels full)	continue assessment	Record keeping of urges to eat beyond scheduled amount or outside scheduled times.
memories of first sex partner	"punished enough; won't get fat"	vomit	Systematize food purchase and consumption	Miles and times (set up schedule for running).
		Possible social skills problems		Do record keeping on best and worst social experience each day.
		suicide attempt	systematize exercise	

Figure 9.2. Preliminary Flow Diagram for a Self-Inducing Vomiter at Intake.

Name F.N. Education University Graduate Marital Status Single Referred by Dr. S. John

Date 3/14/74 Age 21 Occupation Social Work (internship) Presenting Problems Self-induced vomiting and stomach pain.

STIMULI	PRESUMED INTERNAL PROCESSES	TARGET PROBLEMS	TREATMENT METHODS	EVALUATION METHODS
Being alone (not being asked for a date). Social situations.	Self concept: "Large: I tend to get fat; I'm not attractive to most men; I have sinned; I am "soiled goods" and probably unworthy of true love; I am a good runner and would like to run in marathons; I think I could be a good wife and mother; I want to be in control of my life."	Overeating and self-induced vomiting	Systemize food purchase and consumption	Keep records of urges (+ occasions) to eat beyond the scheduled amounts and record vomiting episodes.
		Client is alone - usually on Friday or Saturday evenings; urge to eat	Daily exercise (marathon training with the club coach) in late afternoon	
Memories of a series of enjoyable but secret and socially unacceptable sex experiences	"Lonely, unloved; rejected because I'm too fat; angry."	Purchases and eats large quantities of doughnuts, cake, bread	Medical management, dietary management (exercise has been approved)	Keep daily records on weight, food purchase, eating and exercising (miles and times, refer to schedule set up by coach).
	"Tense; guilty, unworthy; soiled goods."	Feels full and uncomfortable (feels even more fat)	Progressive relaxation	Medical reassessment in 3 months.

with a married man who has moved across the continent.

Any unpleasant experience.

Vomiting discovered on 2/25/74

After vomiting client feels less likely to get fat (the calories are gone) and less uncomfortable and guilty ("somehow the suffering of vomiting atones for my sins"); "I don't want anyone to know I've sinned or that I vomit."

Depression

Anxiety

Induces vomiting with finger

Stomach pains (for the last 6 months; most intense in social situations)

Social Behavior (seems agitated and curt; avoids close relationships by being rude when she feels attracted to someone)

Suicide attempt on 2/27/74

Biofeedback (SCL, temp) for control of autonomic function

Social skills training

Individual psychotherapy

Use pain questionnaire for keeping records of stomach pain episodes, and pain medication taken.

Weekly Rathus and daily record keeping of best and worst social experiences.

Weekly Zung index of depression.

Figure 9.3. *Flow diagram for vomiter after four sessions.*

I have omitted some details from Figures 9.1 through 9.3 in order to present the format more clearly. We include a general Self-Concept section in the "Presumed Internal Processes" column. Here we list the client's descriptions of his or her interests, strengths, weaknesses, and other salient characteristics. In the Treatment Method column, we often indicate the sequence of the different treatments we are planning, estimate the number of sessions for each treatment procedure, and indicate the evaluation criteria that will determine whether a particular procedure should be continued beyond the estimated number of sessions.

Ms. N's flow diagrams – and flow diagrams in general – do not address all aspects of the shifty theory of personality (as shown in Figure 3.1); they do address the aspects of Ms. N's life that seemed the most important and the most in need of attention. As Ms. N improved, we composed new versions of her diagram.

By now it should come as no surprise that our flow diagrams for other clients with bulimia are very different from Ms. N's. Many of the others include a sizable role for the interplay of SNS activity and central motive state.

Other Uses

The flow diagram is compatible with the ABC approach to understanding clients (outlined in Chapter 8). The ABC can be used to develop separate initial descriptions for each of the problems presented by the client, along with descriptions of various aspects of the biopsychosocial forces involved in an episode of problem behavior (examples are given in other chapters). The ABC strategy can also be used in the initial interview and in preliminary communications with consultants and referring agents. The basic ABC diagram does not permit inclusion of general descriptions of internal processes or the matching of assessment and treatment procedures to the various problems. But the obvious temporal sequence ("flow") of the ABC diagram can easily be incorporated into the flow diagram format; the arrows in Figure 9.3 indicate some of our hypotheses about temporal sequences.

Finally, the flow diagram format facilitates communication with consultants and collaborators from outside the mental health professions. The various medical procedures of assessment and treatment are conveniently described and scheduled on the same page with the psychotropic medications and psychotherapy or behavioral therapy. I also use the flow diagram when I make presentations at case conferences. Chapter 13 contains many examples of flow diagrams.

Client as Coinvestigator

I have found that the relationship between the therapist and the client, and the client's attitude toward the therapeutic effort are often fostered and supported by enlisting the client as a personal scientist/theorist, or coinvestigator. For example, at the end of the first session, most clients can be given a record-keeping assignment that is tailored to their particular presenting problem. At the very least, the client might be asked to log the status of his or her presenting complaint once per day, between suppertime and bedtime. Or a phobic client might log the number of panic attacks that had occurred since the previous meal was taken; this could be done three times per day, before each meal. For each panic attack, he or she would note the situation and the severity of the panic on a scale of 1 to 5. (Tying these observations to a specific, routine behavior such as eating increases the chance that the forms are filled out.) Or one might ask that the client record only a description of the most anxiety-provoking or most enjoyable experience of the day. Whatever the schedule for recording, the client brings the record-keeping sheet to each session for discussion. The client's sense of self-control and responsibility can be enhanced by becoming a coinvestigator in this manner.

Evaluation Issues

We often encounter the problem of needing baseline data against which to judge therapeutic interventions, while the client's clinical needs may demand that treatment (and record keeping) be started immediately. In such cases we use the "retrospective baseline" method proposed by Houtler and Rosenberg (1985). Basically, during a very early interview, we collect as much information as possible concerning the variables in question (such as severity of symptoms, number of incidents of maladaptive behavior) during, say, the previous four weeks. We obtain this information carefully, often not only from the client, but also from significant others or from previously-written critical incident reports. At regular intervals throughout treatment, or at least at the end of treatment, we then obtain similar retrospective information, using exactly the same procedures as we used during the collection of the retrospective baseline. While bias cannot be eliminated in this way, at least the data points are more or less compatible, and the client is spared a possibly unethical delay in needed treatment.

The flow-diagram format is easy to use and easy to adapt as shifts occur. Without it, I would be less effective.

10 : Biofeedback

"Biofeedback" is a catchy modern label for a process that has been used by generations of psychophysiologists exploring the interface between psychological and biological functions.

As early as 1898, Allan M. Cleghorn (the father of Robert Cleghorn who was my post doctoral advisor) described a blood-pressure feedback device. Cleghorn's device was the size of a fire hydrant and was used to give blood pressure information back to the patient being monitored. Many others in the nine decades since then have described various feedback devices and methods – but the term biofeedback did not enter the language until about 17 years ago. In 1973, some colleagues and I published an article we entitled, "Instrumental Control of Autonomic Responses with the Use of a Cognitive Strategy" (Corson et al., 1973). I can't remember if we had heard the word biofeedback by then. In any event, the expression has since won out and is certainly more memorable than the terminology used in our 1973 article.

Indeed, part of the problem with biofeedback is that the term is catchy and that the concept can be oversimplified. It is important to recognize that there are both problems and limitations – as well as possibilities – in the application of biofeedback procedures.

General Method

Biofeedback works by detecting, amplifying, and translating an aspect of biological function into a form that can be interpreted by the individual whose biological processes are being monitored. The process of biofeedback thus involves three operations, as shown in

Figure 10.1.

(1)   Detection of a biological process that would otherwise be difficult or impossible for the subject to perceive.
(2)   Transduction of the targeted biological process to a signal, which is amplified and modulated.
(3)   Feedback of the signal to the subject, who uses the signal to perceive and control the biological process producing the signal.

The subject can learn not only to sense the targeted biological process (or its correlates), but also to control it – if the signal being fed back is meaningful and corresponds to changes in the underlying biological process.

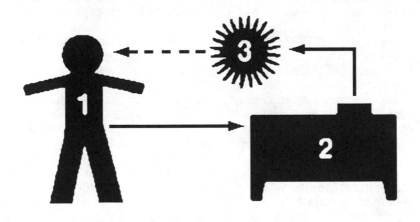

Figure 10.1. *The Biofeedback Loop.*

The information provided in biofeedback procedures can take many forms. In some applications, biofeedback provides information that the subject can use in much the way visual feedback is used to control accuracy while throwing a ball or shooting an arrow. In other applications, the focus is on the timing of the activity, such as when a musician learns to play within the rhythmic constraints of an unfamiliar musical group. In still other applications, biofeedback can help achieve the integration of complex processes, such as when the respiratory and the skeletal musculature must be coordinated in order to learn to swim.

In addition, biofeedback can make different uses of the information being fed back. In some applications, the biofeedback is the equivalent of reward; in others, it is the equivalent of an error signal. In some cases, biofeedback acts as a continuous information source, providing guidance for the honing of a skill; in other situations, biofeedback functions more as a discrete incentive event that occurs only when a successful response is made.

Control of the underlying biological process may also take several forms. In electromyography, or measurement of the intrinsic electrical properties of skeletal muscle, for instance, the goal may be to change the absolute level of muscle tension. In treating some forms of hypertension, on the other hand, the goal may be to minimize variations in the blood pressure. The following clinical examples will clarify the importance of distinguishing between *levels* in the biological process and *episodes* of change in the biological process being studied.

An Application with Pain and Spasms

My first clinical example here involves using clinical psychophysiology[1] and biofeedback to relieve chronic pain and muscle spasm. A 48-year-old man with total paralysis below the mid chest, resulting from an injury four years prior to admission, was referred to the Psychology Section at the White River Junction Veterans Hospital for treatment of chronic pain and severe muscle spasms. He was interviewed and administered the Dartmouth Pain Questionnaire (Corson and Schneider, 1984), a brief, six-part questionnaire. This work-up served to identify the locations of his chronic pain and to establish the fact that severe muscle spasms occurred in response to unexpected noises – sometimes as little as a click from a ballpoint pen. The spasms began in areas where the

[1] This chapter focuses on biofeedback – and touches on non-biofeedback applications of clinical psychophysiology only insofar as they are related to the biofeedback applications discussed here. Clinical psychophysiology is a large and active field that is only narrowly addressed here.

client said he was in constant pain. Psychophysiological assessment using three electromyography (EMG) machines showed that his spasms could be traced from muscle groups that were involved early (two to six seconds after auditory stimulus) to those involved later (seven to 14 seconds after auditory stimulus). We were also able to identify an electrodermal orienting response – a slight increase in electrical conductance of the skin, which indicates autonomic arousal – that reliably preceded the EMG activation and spasm.

On the basis of these observations, we designed a biofeedback treatment that "uncoupled" the skeletal from the autonomic responses. The treatment took 15 sessions and involved two phases. The first phase took nine sessions of 45 minutes each in which the client lowered his EMG and electrodermal activity levels while monitoring analog, or dial-type, feedback.

The second phase of the treatment took six sessions, in which a combination of analog and binary feedback was used. For the first three minutes in these sessions, the client attempted to lower his EMG using analog feedback once again. Following this three-minute period, a binary – or simple on-off readout – EMG threshold was set just above the lowest point attained during the period of analog feedback. The client was then instructed to keep his muscles relaxed enough not to trigger the binary EMG signal (a tone). In other words, following the three minutes of unidirectional EMG training a binary threshold was set; then bidirectional electrodermal training was begun. Now the client was asked to first raise the electrodermal tone (using arousing imagery) for 90 seconds, and then to lower the tone for 90 seconds (using relaxation strategies and strategies developed during the previous biofeedback training). In the event that the EMG tone was triggered, the electrodermal feedback was terminated until 20 seconds after the client had relaxed enough to turn the EMG tone off.

A short test – with no biofeedback – was conducted at the beginning and end of each of these 15 sessions. The instructions for this test were as follows: "Now please raise arousal (electrodermal activity) to a point just below that which would trigger a spasm." By the 10th session, the number of spasms during test periods had dropped to zero. The client's overall daily spasm frequency followed a similar pattern: spasm frequency dropped from over 100 per day (a rate documented by EMG monitoring) to zero. Follow-up five years later showed that this effect persisted.

Other Applications

There are many other applications for biofeedback techniques. In some medical situations, biofeedback may be the treatment of choice. For instance, a client suffering fecal incontinence may have lost, or failed to develop, properly-timed and integrated control of the internal and external sphincter muscles. Clients with this condition fail to integrate the sensation of fullness in the bowel with proper timing of relaxations and contractions of the sphincter muscles.

A balloon inserted in the bowel allows the therapist to vary the pressure in order to teach the client the sensation of having a full bowel. Other balloons or pressure-sensitive devices are inserted in the internal and external sphincters, and feedback traces from these muscles inform the client of the activity of the sphincter muscles. Using these traces as a guide, the client is able to acquire skill at contracting and relaxing these muscles in response to changes in pressure in the bowel.

In this application, biofeedback provides a sensory prosthesis as well as a guide to the acquisition of particular muscle skills. The client is able to integrate the sensory and muscular components required to gain control over an otherwise intractable clinical problem.

Biofeedback has also been used successfully in the treatment of several conditions in which the client learns to gain control of pathophysiological processes not ordinarily under voluntary control. Headache caused by vasospasm or muscle tension, for example, sometimes can be relieved by biofeedback. Raynaud's disease, characterized by vasospasm in response to cold or emotional arousal, has been treated successfully by training the client to maximize blood flow in the peripheral blood vessels. Likewise, biofeedback has been used in the treatment of respiratory problems such as reactive hyperventilation and continuing dependence on a respirator (Corson et al.,1976); in the rehabilitation of stroke victims needing retraining of skeletal muscles; and in control of such autonomic disturbances as hyperhidrosis, or excessive perspiration. Of particular interest here, biofeedback has also been used with behavioral and psychological problems. Biofeedback is particularly helpful when symptoms include a clear physiological component. In anxiety-based panic attacks, for example, the underlying pathology may be psychological, but dramatic physiological signs are reliably present – sweating, dizziness, racing heartbeat, and so forth. These are so distressing to the client that they compound and perpetuate the anxiety, and they can also lead to further physical problems. Biofeedback has been used to alleviate the physiological signs and thereby to reduce the psychological pathology as well.

Athletes have been trained to maximize performance using biofeedback. The members of the Canadian military biathlon team underwent biofeedback training in addition to regular training to maximize their performance in a sport combining cross-country skiing with rifle target shooting. The team members were trained to lower their arousal rapidly after a period of racing and to squeeze the trigger only between heartbeats. As a result, the Canadian biathletes went from being perennial also-rans to world champions.

Evaluation

It is relatively easy to measure the improvement in athletic performance as a result of biofeedback training. However, clinical examples involving such singular skill acquisition, in which biofeedback is the only treatment used, and where the target problem is easy to measure are not common. Generally, the biofeedback trainer relies on (1) measures of pre- and post-treatment skill level, (2) measures of biological function taken during a training session, or (3) client reports of changes in the frequency, amplitude, or duration of the target behavior, feeling, or process. The problem of fecal incontinence is one that does have a simple, objective, and measurable outcome. However, problems of general anxiety disorders are not as easy to monitor.

One problem in obtaining a reliable measure of results is that the various domains of measurement do not always correlate. Measured levels of physiological responses may be at variance with the client's subjective report or with overt behavior. In treating the behavioral problem of stuttering, for instance, observed speaking fluency may not correlate well with physiological arousal or subjective report.

The complexities of individual differences and variations in situational triggers of problems likewise confound studies of results in the therapeutic setting. Nonetheless, several avenues are currently being explored, including psychological and psychophysiological profiling, to evaluate clients' responses to standardized situations.

Another problem arises as a result of the fact that biofeedback usually is not used alone. Often biofeedback is one technique in a package of modalities. The fact that biofeedback may be adjunctive to several other procedures makes it difficult to measure the singular impact of the biofeedback – or of any other single component of the treatment program.

To what extent, people often wonder, does biofeedback permanently "rewire" the client – or is continuing practice necessary?

Rewiring probably does not occur – but may seem to occur in cases where continuing practice is assured or automatic. For example, continuing practice is assured in cases of fecal incontinence; if the newly acquired skills are not practiced, a clear failure signal results. Similarly, when a partially paralyzed client is weaned from a respirator and taught to breathe independently, failure to perform the necessary maneuvers is clearly signaled to the client by feelings of dizziness and other signs of respiratory insufficiency.

Practice Issues

In other applications of biofeedback, the necessity for continuing practice is not as easily signaled to the client. In these cases, the clinician must maintain contact with the client for months after the skill has been acquired to insure regular practice and proper use of the skill. Two examples illustrate the complexity of this issue.

The first involved healthy college students trained to control their autonomic levels by way of electrodermal biofeedback. No change was noticed in their cardiovascular response to a painful stimulus – unless they intended to use the acquired skill. When the subjects were not thinking about using the skill, their heart rate and blood pressure rose to the same levels as prior to training. However, when they intentionally used the acquired skill during the application of a painful stimulus, they were able to significantly reduce their heart rate, blood pressure, and sensation of pain.

The second example involves clinical application of autonomic biofeedback (skin conductance) to the treatment of muscle spasms. In my experience, clients must continue practicing in order to maintain a reduction in the frequency of spasms. If they do not continue to practice, the frequency, amplitude, or duration of spasms will regress toward pretreatment baseline levels. The question of skill level is complex. During the days after practice is terminated and spasms are returning to the pretreatment level, clients have come back to the treatment setting to have their skills measured. By the best available measures, clients' skills were intact in the laboratory. But the skills were not sufficient to give persisting relief in the real world.

Other Problems

These problems – measurement of skill acquisition and ensuring the maintenance of those skills – are but two difficult issues facing biofeedback researchers and practitioners. Other issues include:

(1) Some disorders readily lend themselves to biofeedback treatment while others do not.
(2) People differ widely in their self-concept and in their sense of themselves as agents capable of controlling important aspects of their lives.
(3) People differ dramatically in their ability to learn and to profit from biofeedback training (this is not simply a question of differences in intelligence).
(4) People differ in their willingness to learn (perhaps because of a desire to maintain the sick role or to receive disability payments).
(5) Successful treatment with biofeedback is often mistakenly accepted as proof that the problem was "simply psychosomatic" or "all in your head."
(6) Even successfully treated clients vary in their ability and willingness to practice the skills that brought them relief, and a rusty skill when called upon in an emergency is almost doomed to fail.
(7) Different practitioners – perhaps depending on their training or on the kinds of cases they see – give widely varying emphasis to biofeedback techniques in their treatment programs, so that it is often difficult to determine the effectiveness of a particular technique or intervention.
(8) The manifestation of the clinical problem may sometimes be confusing (for example, it may be reactive to a baffling array of life situations, and not reliable in its reactivity to any single life situation).
(9) The problems with which biofeedback must deal are complex human and medical problems, so that failures or partial successes are more likely than dramatic and complete triumphs.

Whether biofeedback is better than other simpler treatment

interventions is a complex question. For problems like some forms of fecal incontinence, in which there are clear physiological or behavioral factors to shape, biofeedback appears to be the treatment of choice. For other problems, such as tension headaches, the answer is not clear. (These issues are reviewed by Hatch et al., 1987.)

Compared with relaxation training, biofeedback seems to have a higher yield: more clients continue to attend sessions and persist in practicing their skills. Whether this is because of a placebo effect or due to a heightened expectancy of what the high-technology device will do for them is not clear. More research is needed to define criteria for client selection and for appropriate problems to be treated with biofeedback.

We must work to define the relationships between the specific features of clients and the variations in their success at acquiring skills from biofeedback training. This need is dramatized by the observation of powerful relationships between personality and differences in reactivity to success and failure signals.

The general issues involved in sorting out the reward and the information components of the biofeedback signal – as well as the technical issues involved in the modality of feedback and the spacing of feedback signals – also need to be addressed.

A Technique for Profiling

Among the most exciting prospects for the future of biofeedback and clinical psychophysiology is that of psychophysiological profiling. The evaluation of psychophysiological responses to standardized stimuli can help (1) select a treatment modality, (2) monitor the impact of ongoing treatment, and (3) assess the long-term effect of treatment.

My colleagues and I have developed a 12-minute sequence to do this, involving a five-minute period of relaxation, 30 seconds of submersion of the nondominant hand (up to the wrist) in ice water, a one-minute evaluation of verbal skills, 30 more seconds of submersion of the nondominant hand in ice water, and five more minutes of relaxation.

Preliminary analyses of results with hundreds of individuals indicate that there are consistencies and differences in physiological and subjective response to this test. With further progress in sorting out these differential responses, we will be better able to tailor intervention and evaluation techniques to the needs of individual clients and conditions. The procedure has been incorporated into the multimodality format for violent clients that is described in Chapter 12.

11 : A Selective Literature Review

I have organized this selective review of the literature around the dimensions that I use to describe the violent episodes of our clients. Important dimensions of a client's typical violent outbursts are the stressors or triggers that may have provoked the outburst and the working self-concept that was apparently active at the time of the outburst. (Table 11.1 operationalizes these and other dimensions into a series of continua.) Initially, I developed the continua to describe our own clients and the differences among them (as in Chapter 12). I have since used these continua to help me compare our violent clients with clients described in the literature.

This comparison helped me to identify a gap. Most severely violent clients described in the literature are housed in custodial institutions (prisons and hospitals), while the less severely violent are not institutionalized; the typical client referred to us is not institutionalized, but is more severely violent than the noninstitutionalized clients described in the literature. Our clients are also from lower socioeconomic levels than the violent outpatients typically described in the literature. In effect, therefore, the literature to date has rarely described clients like ours living in circumstances like ours. Hence, a selective review of the literature is warranted. Moreover, some excellent and recent reviews can be cited. We need not traverse any ground that has so recently been well covered.

Table 11.1

Continua on Which Episodes of Violent Behavior can be Characterized

Sudden	Slow
Unprovoked	Provoked
Undirected	Directed
Unpredictable	Predictable
Unstoppable	Stoppable
Patient will stop self short of causing injury to the target	Patient will not stop self short of causing severe injury to the target
Patient will stop when others intervene verbally	Patient will not stop unless totally physically restrained
Unplanned	Planned
No memory	Memory
Remorse	No remorse
Not righteous	Righteous
No reason(s)/stimulus(i) cited	Reason(s)/stimulus(i) cited
No values cited	Societal, religious, or personal values cited
Stressors/triggers not identifiable	Stressors/triggers identifiable
Control issues not involved	Control issues involved
No audience necessary	Audience usually present
Short duration (lasts seconds)	Long duration (lasts hours)
Subject expresses displeasure	Subject expresses pleasure (before, during or after)
Not verbal	Verbal
Physical	Not physical
Life-threatening	Not life-threatening
Not directed at (an) object(s)	Directed at (an) object(s)
Not directed at a person or animal	Directed at a person or animal
Constant pattern	Variable pattern
Overcontrolled	Undercontrolled (also subcultural)
Drive mediated	Instrumental

Neurological Correlates

The extreme, dangerous, and sudden explosions of violent behavior that generally lead to institutionalization have often been equated with a condition known as episodic dyscontrol. At the behavioral level, the term episodic dyscontrol is usually reserved for individuals with a history of violent outbursts upon little or no provocation. Although the term implies a neurological substrate, some confusion surrounds the neurological correlates of the condition.

Among the neurological studies conducted on people meeting the behavioral definition, neurological results conflict even when one looks at studies with similar methodology (Riley and Niedermeyer, 1977; Hughes and Hermann, 1984). Elliott (1982) studied a sample of 245 subjects with histories of uncontrollable rage upon little or no provocation and found that about 40 percent of these individuals showed no EEG abnormalities. Such findings may be related to technical problems, such as relying on recordings from scalp electrodes rather than on recordings from subcortical structures (Smith, 1980), or relying on recordings taken only during quiescent periods. On the other hand, the findings may indicate that no fundamental brain abnormalities are related to the violent outbursts of some people. As far as I can now see, we must consider the relationship between episodic violent behavior and specific pathology of the central nervous system to be an open question.

Another neurological process does appear reliably correlated, and it may even become a reliable predictor of violent outbursts. This, as discussed in Chapter 3, is the sudden activation of the SNS, or the sympathetic branch of the autonomic nervous system. In fact, the literature on central nervous system abnormalities that are correlated with violent outbursts contains frequent mention of pronounced signs of sympathetic hyperactivity (Stone et al., 1986). Our own data (described in Chapter 3) provide solid support for this observation. Specifically, we have never seen an exception to the following statement: in violent clients, SNS arousal, as indexed by upward shifts in skin conductance, correlates with the client recounting situations that provoked anger or violent behavior. Numerous other investigators have observed such correlations between autonomic function and violent behavior. Recently, Van der Kolk and Greenberg (1987) summarized much of the literature on this relationship and offered a number of observations and suggestions that are compatible with my own experiences and ideas. In the following paragraphs, I will relate their observations and others' to some of the more important aspects of assessing and treating violent clients.

Early Environment

I will not review the possibility that a separate genetic bias toward violent behavior might occur in some people; support exists for this possibility, and it has recently been reviewed (Holden, 1987). We will focus instead on the environmental determinants that I have been developing in the preceding chapters.

One general environmental cause for the neurological impairment that can lead to violent behavior can be quickly identified. Violent adults are likely to have been physically abused as children (Heath et al., 1986; Eron, 1987). The medial temporal structures, which are more susceptible to injury than those in other brain locations (MacLean, 1986), are the structures that have a high probability of showing abnormalities in violent individuals.

Other identified environmental determinants of adult violent behavior are nonphysical. Table 11.1 includes several labels for aggressive behavior (subcultural and instrumental) that imply emulation of parents and others who have been observed using aggressive or violent behaviors to obtain desired outcomes or objects. Eron (1987) and others have made a very strong case for the contribution of emulation or modeling to the development of adult violent behavior. In Chapter 14 we will consider another possible learned pathway to development of adult violent behavior – one based on negative reinforcement, on learning to be violent in order to terminate aversive stimuli.

In Chapter 13, when we consider the case histories of four clients, we will see that in some clients, all of these environmental causes appear to converge.

Hyperarousal and The Binary Switch

Van der Kolk and Greenberg (1987) cite evidence that an abusive early environment can contribute to the development of hyperarousal states that will have long-term detrimental effects on the child's ability (and later the adult's ability) to modulate both anxiety and aggression. This chronic hyperarousal state in traumatized persons "often causes them to go immediately from stimulus to response" (Van der Kolk and Greenberg, 1987, page 66). The sudden overreaction to even minor stimuli as if they were emergency situations has been characterized as an "all-or-nothing" response pattern. The all-or-nothing response, the sudden transition from stimulus to major response without apparent internal dialogue, characterizes most of the violent clients whom I have seen.

In reconstructing some episodes of violent explosion with most clients, one does see evidence of internal dialogue. Most of this dialogue appears to involve pre- or postviolence rehearsal of the expectancies and dispositions that lead to the "binary switch" or the all-or-nothing explosive response. Eron (1987) supports this observation in his summary of a longitudinal study of the development of aggression: "Over the 22 years of this study, it was what the subjects were saying to themselves about what they wanted, what their environment would permit or expect, what might be an effective or appropriate response, and what were the likely consequences of such action that helped determine how aggressive they are today (page 441)." The repetition of such well-practiced internal dialogue facilitates the observed automaticity and rapidity of transition from stimulus to response. On this point, Goldfried says, "Because of the habitual nature of one's expectations or beliefs it is likely that the thinking processes and images become automatic and seemingly involuntary like most overlearned acts (in Staub, 1980 page 324)."

Many reports of successful therapy with violent individuals have focused on developing new forms of internal dialogue. On the other hand (as already mentioned several times), most of the clients I have worked with appear unable to pause between stimulus and response for internal dialogue until considerable work is done in training them to monitor and to modulate the emotional fire in their boiler.

Level-Setting Functions of the ANS

As mentioned in Chapter 3, the autonomic nervous system (ANS) appears to perform a level setting and modulating function. This function leads to changes in the probabilities of certain kinds of responses. Van der Kolk and Greenberg (1987) give an excellent example of level setting and modulating mediated by the ANS: "An illustration of the association between autonomic arousal and flashbacks is provided by the case of a former parachutist who had a three-month period of post-traumatic symptoms after his second parachute failed to open during a jump until he was a few hundred feet above the ground. Five years later the only remaining symptom is a flashback of this event after autonomic arousal, such as occurs in a near accident on the road (page 70)." In this case, autonomic arousal appeared to reach a level at which the probability of retrieving a particular memory was dramatically increased.

Such shifts in response probability may be related to either a high chronic resting level of autonomic arousal or to a sudden and high-amplitude autonomic reaction. In most of our violent clients, we have seen both high resting levels and high reactivity. In all of them, we have seen high reactivity (as indexed by skin conductance level). Most reactions, at the outset of treatment, are followed by a long duration of high arousal (i.e., slow recovery). The observation of long-duration episodes of hyperarousal suggests that levels and episodes of activity in the ANS may interact in the violent client. This interaction is depicted in Figures11.1 and 11.2.

Figure 11.1 is hypothetical, an example of a priming effect when successive stimuli are too close together for the system to recover. Figure 11.2 depicts actual data obtained during the assessment of one of our violent clients (Mr. D, who is described in several other chapters). The point is this: in a system that might initially rest at a low level, the inability to recover rapidly from episodes of subpathological autonomic arousal may have the end result of priming the system so that an apparently minor stimulus can produce the all-or-nothing response.

PRE TREATMENT Violent client shows:

1) High resting level.
2) Low input reaction threshold -expectation - more stimuli are processed as threatening.

3) Low output reaction threshold - disposition - more stimuli are overtly reacted to.
4) Fast arousal rise after stimulus.
5) Very slow recovery (slow drop in arousal) after stimulus.

6) Typical starting posture (obvious expectation/disposition) and typical response (threat/attack) rapidly alters environment to alter (↓or↑) provocative power of stimuli.

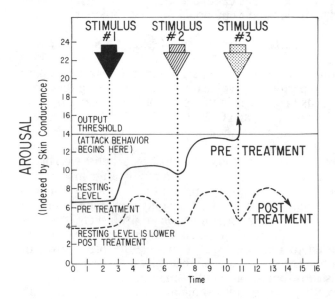

Figure 11.1. *Hypothetical example of the priming effect which occurs when successive stimuli are too close together for the system to recover.*

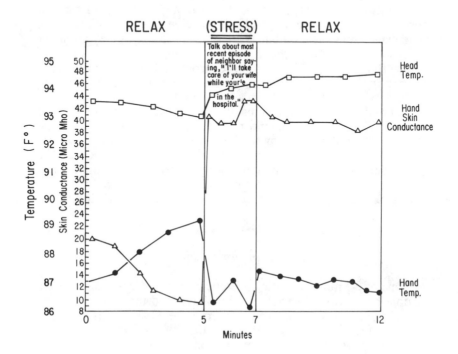

Figure 11.2. *Assessment of an assaultive client.*

In reality, I think I have seen at least three variations on the relationship between arousal levels and episodes of surge in arousal:

(1) The arousal level is chronically high, and minor stimuli always produce violent outbursts.

(2) The moderately high level interacts with episodes of arousal to prime the system as depicted in the accompanying figures.

(3) The level is, relatively, chronically low, but may show a sudden increase to a high level when confronted with certain apparently minor stimuli.

With numerous clients, I have seen what appears to be a progression during treatment through these three stages, and in the order listed. In the third stage, clients are much more selective, in terms of which stimuli they respond to. Even though I may feel that the stimuli are minor, the client will still perceive them as major. In the third stage, the violent outbursts are often as severe as they are in the first stage; however, the duration of the outbursts, and any sub-outburst surges of autonomic arousal, are generally much shorter in duration than those typical of the first stage (when an episode of arousal occurs from a high baseline), or those typical of the second stage (when the episode occurs from a relatively lower baseline). To be helpful to most of the clients I have seen, success must be attained in lowering resting levels of autonomic arousal, in decreasing the duration of episodes of autonomic arousal, and in developing some discrimination among the stimuli that might cause autonomic arousal. Somewhere between the second and third stage, we are able to begin doing effective work with internal dialogue.

Self-Concept

Looking for trouble

One of the most dramatic differences among the members of our sample has involved variables of imagery and tendency to repeat exposing themselves (either in imagery or reality) to stimuli related to the traumatizing event. Many of the clients referred to us for violent outbursts have been Vietnam combat veterans. Van der Kolk and Greenberg (1987) have noted that approximately 20 percent of Vietnam veterans who sought treatment for Posttraumatic Stress Disorder (PTSD) reported that they often exposed themselves to dangerous situations or went to movies that reminded them of their experiences in Vietnam. In some of our clients, the tendency to seek out dangerous situations (such as in taverns or pool halls) has been quite troublesome early in treatment. Several clients have recognized a pattern in the occurrences of their desire to expose themselves to such situations. One Vietnam combat veteran recently told me, "When I began treatment I needed to do it about once every one or two weeks. Now I only do it about once every month, and it's different now. I seem to sit and watch, while before it was like a command performance. Everybody knew I was there and everybody knew something was going to happen. The last two times I went nothing happened." Another veteran told me, "I can go into a strange town and find a place like that within 15 minutes. I can smell it – it's where the action is. I'm like an animal, and when I want to get violent I can always find somebody else who is willing to oblige me.[1] I used to need to do that sometimes."

Both of these individuals were terribly abused as children. One was locked in a closet for at least three days, and the other was locked in a trunk. Both experienced numerous beatings, broken bones, lacerations, and so forth. One was raped by an older male relative, and the other was raped when in a juvenile detention home. Both of these men have verbal IQs above 130. They both have rich fantasy lives and can vividly describe images of combat experiences, of being terrorized and of terrorizing.

These observations are in accord with those of Brett and Ostroff (1985). In considering the relationship between imagery and PTSD, they hypothesize a two-dimensional framework for understanding PTSD based on repetitions and defensive functioning. Indeed, the imagery and behavior of both clients I have just described suggest the presence of a compulsion to repeat trauma-related images and actions and to repeat a definitive form of defensive behavior – namely, violent outbursts. Some of these violent individuals spend much of their time thinking and behaving as if there are only two possible states of themselves – being terrorized or being the terrorist.

The above quotes from clients illustrate the fact that some of these individuals actually look for trouble. The idea that one might feel a need to be violent, to fight, or to be in a dangerous situation has been considered by many authors, and many possible contributing factors have been cited. Terms like "adrenalin junkie" (implying someone who thrives on a high level of adrenalin and ANS arousal), "risk-taker," and "thrill-seeker" have been applied to this behavior.

---

[1] One important aspect of this behavior – discussed further in Chapters 1, 7 and 14 – is the fact that many violent individuals can communicate their readiness for violent behavior to a total stranger in a few seconds without any physical or verbal contact. The violent client assumes a facial expression, a posture, and a gait that communicates to others that he is ready to be violent. This feed forward influence can be observed when some of our clients enter a room full of strangers. In other words, these sometimes subtle behavioral cues regarding a response disposition – a readiness to be violent – are quickly communicated to other people and bias their first response to our clients.

Secondary Gains

The issues regarding looking for trouble are well considered by Horowitz (1981). His theoretical orientation and terminology are very different from those used in this book, but are easily translatable. He points out that violent individuals may persist in this behavior because it is enlivening and provides a type of secondary gain. Horowitz describes one patient:

> The liveliness of the rage extricated him from the states of apathetic dullness so common in narcissistically vulnerable persons. That is, he experienced the rage states as 'fuel' or 'energy'. The rages were idealized and, like an old friend, were embraced to avoid further loss. Only gradually did he learn to enliven himself by healthy, sublimated forms of exhibitionism rather than by reactive rage at being deprived of such pleasures (page 1237).

I am reminded here of Adler's statement that can be roughly paraphrased, "Ask what the symptom or problem does for the client." Sometimes this question pays off well. The prototypical example is where one can identify clear secondary gains for a client, as with the phobic person who maintains control of his or her spouse by the phobic behavior. At other times, this question does not pay off in a simple way, since it seems the symptom/problem is a total loss to the client. And sometimes the symptom or problem both pays off and also hurts the client. Such is the case with most violent clients. The symptom or problem seems an effective short-term way of coping with challenges to self-esteem. To some clients, it even seems an effective short-term way of dealing with any sort of dysphoria.

For most of our clients, the losses are also very clear – loss of trust from other people, alienation from family and former friends, problems with police, inability to hold a job. To realize these losses are occurring entails a recognition of facts that many violent clients are unable or unwilling to acknowledge. Much of the work of treatment focuses on getting these violent individuals to acknowledge the losses. We must train them in the endeavor of becoming personal scientists and theorists, and help them to identify relationships between the essential audience and critic function as these impinge upon their fragile self-esteem.

Critics, Heroes and Monsters

In accord with our own observations, Horowitz (1981) observes that many episodes of self-righteous rage are triggered by injuries to the self-concept or drops in self-esteem. He observes that the states of mind displayed by parents are often emulated by their children, and that certain forms of violent behavior appear to be passed on as styles of emotional expression in a subculture. He attends to the role of parental attention in development of the critic function. It is in this latter area that I find his ideas most helpful. Horowitz describes a specific three-party model or role structure that "contains a hero, a monster, and a critical audience. The critic admires the hero and loathes the monster" (page 1235). This three-party role structure is useful "in understanding why a usually restrained person, when confronted with triggers that instigate this model, may freely express fierce, brutal, but pleasurably exciting hostility. The pleasure is an assumption of dominance over a dehumanized other, a pleasure heightened by feelings of merger with a powerful critic (or group) and exhibition of the self to that critic (or group) to gain attention, admiration, and praise" (page 1235). The locus of the critic function is ambiguous and changing. "Sometimes a given appraisal of blame may be seen as instigated from within and sometimes as instigated from outside of the self. Even when the critical function is located externally, inconsistency is expected as blame is assigned and withdrawn in shifting judgments" (page 1235).

In considering the development of the critic's role, Horowitz says:

> Precursors to the critic's role probably occur during the earliest phases of mother and infant interaction ... [Later in development] the child watches for responses to its behavior – an admiring smile or nod, a gleam in the eye, a scornful look, a pursed mouth, or simply the absence of any response. Parents with changeable mental states and inconsistent styles of response will affect the child differently from those who provide relatively stable reactions to the child's behavior. Eventually, the child watches its own behavior in the manner that had been experienced as parental reflection and criticism ... {In a triad of family interactions} each pair may bond, with some

critical empathy or contempt for the person who is "left out." The patterning of such episodes is internalized, leading the child to learn and revise the critic's role ... If the critic's role patterns are etched more deeply without development of stable autonomous value structures and blame — attribution processes, the person arrives at adulthood with a special vulnerability to labile state changes. This would occur because it is sometimes itself and sometimes the conceptualized other who assigns the self-concept to positions as worthy or unworthy, whole or fragmented, competent or incompetent, to blame or blameless for unleashing evil into the family or group (page 1236).

An extension of these ideas appears valid for my violent clients. Specifically, it appears that the strategies of "get them before they get you" and "always be ready" (which I often hear repeated by these clients) could involve a combination of terror, on the one hand, at possibly being blamed by the critic and joyful anticipation, on the other, of any opportunity to take on the role of hero. And thus ensues their search for despicable monsters and vigilant avoidance, or violent rejection, of any criticism.

Therapeutic Possibilities

With regard to therapeutic procedures, Horowitz says:

Change that is more than the institution of compensatory controls requires a deeper level of analysis. ... [Most therapists] encourage patients to recognize the self-images and self and other schemata by which they organize a situation and the unconscious interpersonal fantasies by which they provoke situations. The addition of the critic's role and the three-party role structure is a subtle but useful supplement to the clear examination of conflicted interpersonal relationship patterns (page 1237).

I suspect that Horowitz would approve of the formats that I have depicted in Figure 1.1 and Table 1.1 in Chapter 1 and Figure 9.1 in Chapter 9. Indeed, he says, "Reconstruction of episodes in the treatment situation usually is necessary also during such examinations of the critic's role" (page 1237). Our specific strategies for this will be spelled out in more detail later. For now, it is worth noting that both Horowitz and I are spending much of our energy considering the assessment and treatment of people who are quite intelligent. The particular strategies he describes, and most of those that I will describe in subsequent chapters are most appropriate for people with at least normal intelligence and verbal skills.

Wong et al. (1987) have described many procedures for use with less intelligent and more regressed individuals. The assessment procedure they use at the outset is similar to that depicted in Table 1.1 of Chapter 1. Because of the limitations of their clients, though, they would be unable to make use of the collaborative and multilevel strategies we have described here. In Chapter 13, I will describe our attempts to make use of these procedures – and some alternatives – with less able individuals.

A New Self-Concept

With some clients, we eventually reach a point where the highly stressful, anger-provoking stimulus must be faced without the easy short-term solution of exploding. Here we must be creative and energetic in developing, with the client, viable alternative responses for dealing with the stimulus and the feelings of upset. We are aided in this endeavor by the realization on the part of the client that he or she now has the ability to detect a high level of the fire in the boiler and to detect some increases, as well as to lower the level and abort the increases.

The interdigitation of the fundamentally biological maneuvers of controlling the fire in the boiler and the fundamentally psychosocial maneuvers of considering and employing other cognitive and overt behaviors in response to this stimulus represent both a new life-style and a new self. As we proceed in therapy with a violent client (as well as with any other client), we must keep constant focus on the evolving transactions between the shifting self-concept and the effect of various stressors. In some cases, we now walk a tightrope. Here I am reminded of some of the stutterers I have treated. In several of them, I could see the reluctance to give up the symptom. One stutterer told me that his stuttering behavior represented a comforting aspect of himself (or a safety signal). Giving up stuttering was to him akin to cutting his ties with "cute little Bobby" and forever casting his lot with "adult Bob." This was at times a terrifying prospect.

At the start of working with some clients referred for violent behavior, I have discussed with them the necessity that they must become willing to lose the power over people that accrues from their reputation as a violent and dangerous person. With some clients, I have discussed the need for them to learn to tolerate humiliation. Needless to say, most are initially reluctant to accept such conditions, and I generally have better luck with these issues later in treatment. Eventually many clients begin to tell me that they have "let an insult pass" or "didn't let it get to me" or "stayed calm;" at this point, I realize that we are on the way to some level of success. Sometimes clients will later describe feeling less powerful, less entitled, less special, less righteous, less ready for anything. When we reach this stage, a fundamental change in self-concept is underway. These changes take many forms and much time. Some aspects of the new self-concept that clients can accept two years after therapy begins would have been very hard for them to even consider at the outset.

Seizures

In this review, I have not yet addressed the treatment possibilities for violent behavior which is related to seizures. For some individuals with seizure-based episodic dyscontrol, a high resting level of activity in the sympathetic nervous system (the fire in the boiler), or a high reactivity, or both, might prime for, or trigger, a seizure. The reciprocally determined relationship between the fire in the boiler and the psychosocial variables, however, suggests that even a client with seizure-based episodic dyscontrol might respond to treatment based solely on psychosocial interventions. Accordingly, Feldman and Paul (1976) video-taped some of their clients' seizures along with the usual psychosocial antecedents, and observed therapeutic benefits of later playing these video-tapes for their clients. One could easily imagine that this experience could help to destigmatize and demystify the seizure event, and clarify the relationship between the seizure and some psychosocial antecedents. The whole process is probably akin to a form of desensitization, which might lead to a lower level of general anxiety, and thus to a lower level of fire in the boiler. The net effect would be to decrease the priming and triggering contributions of the fire in the boiler to the onset of seizure activity. This form of treatment may also help some clients to develop the personal scientist and theorist attitude that aids in developing and using adaptive strategies in all three domains (bio, psycho, and social).

We have used the format shown in Figure 1.1 of Chapter 1 to essentially replicate the procedure of Feldman and Paul with one client who had a seizure disorder (without violent behavior or episodic dyscontrol) that had been caused by a bullet wound to the brain. Our results were consistent with those obtained by Feldman and Paul, and they support the above suggestions regarding the contributions of psychosocial variables and a priming effect of the fire in the boiler. Specifically we observed a reduction in the frequency of seizures and a dramatic reduction in the resting level and lability of the SNS. (These issues are addressed again in Chapter 12.)

Recommended Reading

As I conclude this selective review, I call your attention to two reviews, to a journal that has recently started publication, and to four recent books.

The two reviews cover many of the issues raised here and will provide excellent background on the specific problem of violence and the general problem of therapy/rehabilitation. The first review is a long multiauthor section on violence in an *American Psychiatric Association Annual Review* (Tardiff, 1987). This is multifaceted, thoughtful and broad. One of the most interesting features of this review is the section on "attacks". Attacks (or assaults) that are not motivated by sexual or financial desires, and that do not result in death, are the most frequent forms of violent behavior that psychiatrists deal with. The review points out that they are also the least studied of the violent crimes. Again, it is important to note that attacks of this sort are one of the most frequent problem behaviors of the clients I describe in this book.

The second article, by Gendreau and Ross (1987), reviews the rehabilitation literature from 1981 to 1987. It includes a section on violence and pulls together some promising information on attempts to match rehabilitation strategy to individual differences.

The journal is *Violence and Victims* (published by Springer, beginning in 1986), a valuable reference.

In the first book, Hays et al. (1981) summarize a symposium on "Violence and the Violent Individual" that was held in 1979. This volume provides ideas, theories, methods, data, and legal and ethical considerations regarding violence. The second book, edited by Roth (1987), covers much of the same ground, but is more recent. These two books should be consulted by a reader who wants to obtain a broader view than my narrow and personal account. The third book is a thought provoking effort from Samenow (1987). He addresses the topic of "the criminal mind" with an anecdotal discussion from his work and that of his mentor (Yochelson). Even though the book is uneven, and presents only rare glimpses of an empirical base, it is of value. My impression is that Samenow's criminals bear only a slight resemblance to a few of my violent clients.

Finally, Gaylin (1984) has given us a very personal account of the issues in his widely publicized book, *The Rage Within*. Gaylin's book is a particularly valuable contribution of a sort quite unlike the present volume and unlike anything else I know of in the literature. Gaylin describes many of his own experiences with anger, rage, and violence. In doing so, he validates many of Horowitz's ideas, such as the critic's role and, I feel, he provides support for my general strategy of carefully attending to the specific interactions between stressful situations and working self-concept. Gaylin ends his book with a consideration and elaboration of a position that Freud developed in his later years. The basic idea is that we are locked in a struggle to control and manage anger. In this regard, Freud "embraced the concept of love as man's hope" (page 196). Gaylin's translation of this ends with the idea that Freud meant we must enlarge the population with which we identify. In this way, the population of others (despicable monsters, hostile critics, potential enemies) becomes smaller, while the population of us expands. "In doing so we magnify ourselves, and reduce our sense of vulnerability" (page 196).

12 : Population, Treatment Method, and Results

In this chapter, I will review the characteristics of our population of violent adults. You will then read about assessment and treatment methods that my colleagues and I have used with these and other clients. Finally, I will describe results, with an emphasis on physiological and behavioral findings with a smaller sample of violent clients on whom we recently obtained follow-up data.

The total population consists of 113 men and two women referred for outbursts of violent behavior (physical assault on a person or object). These people were referred to the Psychology Section at the White River Junction (VT) Veterans Administration Hospital between 1974 and 1984. Of the 115, I had enough personal contact with 62 of the men to gather details about their histories and to follow most aspects of their assessment and treatment.

The original 115 clients were all military veterans, mostly from the lower to middle socioeconomic classes, and they had an average of ten years of education. More than half of them had been in trouble with the law for assault. Of these 115, 41 reported having made some sort of physical assault on another person during the week before beginning treatment. And 35 of the 115 clients were reported to have beaten someone to unconsciousness. Public fist-fights were very frequent in this group of clients, and many had spent considerable time in jail on charges including assault, armed robbery, and murder.

Sample

Table 11.1 in Chapter 11 shows the continua that I use to

characterize violent clients; reference to these continua will assist us in this general description of the 62 people I am most familiar with.

The first continuum, *sudden/slow*, pertains to the development of the violent behavior from the point of view of an observer, as do the second and third – *unprovoked/provoked* and *undirected/ directed*. On these first three continua, our subjects typically show sudden, provoked, and directed episodes.

On the fourth continuum – *unpredictable/predictable* – their behavior is usually predictable, both by themselves and by an observer who has some experience with the client's prior behavior.

On the continuum *stoppable/unstoppable*, and the two following ones defining the conditions for stopping, our clients vary. Some of them (like Mr. A, described in Chapter 13) show the pattern of not stopping until either he or the other person is unconscious, or unless he is completely restrained. However, many of our clients, in at least some episodes, have shown the ability to stop as soon as the opponent submits or "gives up."

With regard to the continuum *unplanned/planned*, the episodes vary. Most episodes show some signs of being briefly planned; they also show signs of being well practiced and even rehearsed, perhaps both overtly and in imagination.

On the continuum *no memory/memory*, almost all of the episodes of all clients are clearly remembered. No client in this sample has remembered less than half of his violent outbursts.

As for *remorse/no remorse*, most show no remorse. This corresponds with findings for the next three continua – *not righteous/righteous, no reason(s)/reasons, no values/values*. Most episodes are followed by righteous justification, with reasons cited and some form of value cited, usually societal or personal.

On the next two continua – stressors, triggers *not identifiable/ identifiable*, and control issues *not involved/involved* – stressors or triggers are always identifiable, and control issues are often involved.

Concerning *no audience necessary/audience usually present*, I believe an "essential audience" with its "critic function" is always present, even when the client destroys an object with no one else around. In fact, most of the violent episodes that caused these clients to be referred to me occurred in public, with one or more observers present.

On the next continuum – *short duration/long duration* – even when the violent behavior lasts for a very short time, the feelings of anger and violent urges may last for hours, or even days.

As for *subject expresses displeasure/subject expresses pleasure*, these clients often expressed displeasure immediately before and during the violent episode; the displeasure would be expressed as if it were about the behavior of some despicable monster. But when the episode has ended my clients typically express pleasure with their own heroic behavior and righteous attitudes. Some would go even further and actually express feeling joy while being violent. One of the subjects described in Chapter 13 (Mr. B) recalled an episode of his violent behavior as a "spiritual orgasm"; while I'm not sure exactly what he means by that, I can assume there was some joy involved.

On the next two continua – *not verbal/verbal* and *physical/not physical* these clients are much more likely to get into trouble for showing physical than verbal violence, but most of them are also well practiced in delivering verbal abuse.

On the continuum of *life threatening/not life threatening*, at least some episodes of more than half of these 62 clients have been life threatening, and indeed many of these people have been responsible for the deaths of others. However, even in those individuals who show the most severely life-threatening forms of violent outbursts, the vast majority of their outbursts do not result in loss of life.

The next two continua are *not directed at object/directed at object* and *not directed at a person or animal/directed at a person or animal*. Many of the violent behaviors are aimed at another person, but a very high percentage also involve objects. For example, several of my clients have attacked their own houses with chain saws, and their own cars with sledge hammers. On the other hand, very few violent episodes (except in the case of one client) are directed at animals.

As for the continuum *constant/variable*, most of my clients show several sorts of violent behavior, with at least some of them being quite reliable in pattern, and others showing high degrees of variability.

The last two continua in Table 11.1 – *overcontrolled/undercontrolled* and *drive-mediated/instrumental* – require some elaboration. The continuum of *overcontrolled/ undercontrolled* (Megargee, 1966) is related to issues of modeling and subculture. Undercontrolled violence is typical of individuals whose parents, relatives, neighbors and peers expressed positive attitudes about violent behavior. Masters, Burish, Hollon, and Rimm (1987) point out that these undercontrolled clients are the most difficult to work with. On the other hand, overcontrolled violence is the sort one would see in a person who was brought up in an entirely different cultural setting, who struggles to control violent urges, and who explodes only rarely. The final continuum – *drive mediated/instrumental* (Feshbach, 1970) is also related to cultural issues, but not as clearly as the previous continuum. The prototypical example of instrumental violence occurs in service of obtaining some desired object. On the other hand, the prototypical example of drive-mediated violence occurs in service of intense emotion.

Most of these clients (with no more than five exceptions) typically show undercontrolled and drive-mediated violence. A few had histories of some episodes of instrumental violence (e.g., armed robbery), but such episodes are vastly outnumbered by episodes of drive-mediated violence.

These last two continua mix in a complex way with many of my clients. Their acts of violence are instrumental in developing and keeping their "dangerous" reputations. These reputations are protective and important to their self-concepts and involve issues such as pride and masculinity. Thus it is that *instrumental, undercontrolled* and *drive mediated* may all describe the same act.

From the above descriptions, you now have an idea about who these clients are. But a final note with regard to episodic dyscontrol is in order. Of the 62 clients I know best, 25 have had at least one neurological evaluation with an EEG, and only nine of these show any neurological abnormality. Only one of the four clients described in Chapter 13 has a documented neurological abnormality that shows up in the EEG, although all four were subjected to numerous neurological exams with EEG.

Assessment and Treatment Methods

With my colleagues, I have designed and evaluated a multimodal assessment and treatment program for clients showing violent behavior. The program includes various techniques – relaxation training, biofeedback, and elements of systematic desensitization and various strategies of cognitive behavior therapy, including "stress innoculation" (Meichenbaum, 1977). Other investigators have reported some success with one or several of these techniques (e.g., Goodwin and Mahoney, 1975), but none have used biofeedback of autonomic activity in the way that we have, and none have attempted to influence all three realms (bio, psycho, and social) of the clients' lives in the way that we have. Furthermore, as mentioned earlier, our sample of clients is unlike any sample of outpatients with which extensive use of roughly comparable procedures has been evaluated. We have used variations on this program with all 115 of our population of violent clients, and the sequence has been essentially standardized over the past six years. (Individual treatment variations will be spelled out in Chapter 13.)

The program has three phases. Most of the program and its elements are applicable to clients with problems other than violent behavior. Where I have included a special technique for the violent client, I will so indicate in the discussion.

Phase I

Phase I consists of a behavioral interview and a psycho-physiological assessment (stress profile). The interview identifies the stimuli that trigger the individual's violent episodes (or other stress reactions) and his or her characteristic biological, emotional, behavioral, and cognitive responses.

I obtain informed consent prior to the psychophysiological assessment. This assessment entails monitoring autonomic activity (as indexed by at least two variables – electrodermal activity and finger temperature) during the 12-minute relaxation-stress-relaxation sequence that was described in Chapter 10. The variable that shows the greater change is then picked as the more suitable physiological variable for the subsequent biofeedback (in all cases described here electrodermal activity was selected). The psychophysiological assessment also establishes one of the baselines for eventual evaluation of the impact of treatment.

At the first and at each subsequent session, detailed reports are obtained from the client regarding some specific behavioral and subjective variables. For this purpose, I use the general format shown in Figures 12.1a and 12.1b. When I am assessing a violent client, I also obtain detailed reports regarding anger felt and expressed during the prior 24 hours. (Specifically, the report format determines if clients felt or expressed anger; threatened, grabbed, pushed, or hit anyone; or hit anyone until they or the other person became unconscious. The strategy depicted in Table 1.1 of Chapter 1 is used for this purpose, along with a general questioning strategy that is tailored for the client and for the situation being described.)

At the end of the first and each subsequent session, the clients are asked to keep a daily record, to be filled in between suppertime and bedtime, of one of the following:

Figure 12.1a *Data gathering format for use at outset of each session (side a).*

Corson
Dartmouth College
1988

Scale 0=None, 3=Moderate, 5=Highest

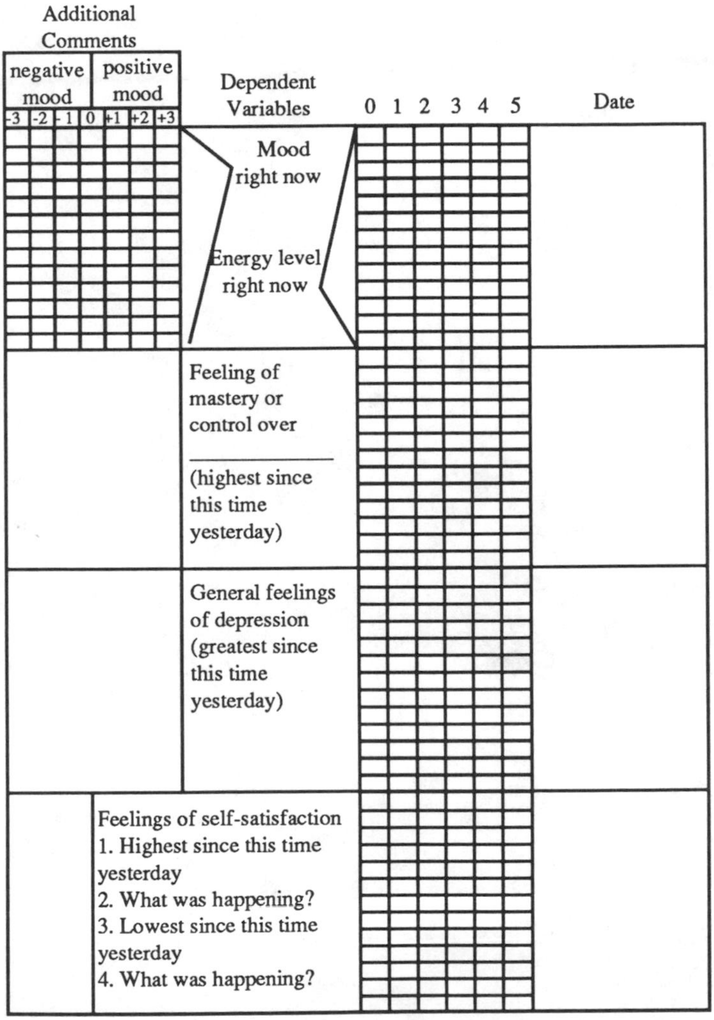

Additional Comments								Dependent Variables	0 1 2 3 4 5	Date
negative mood			positive mood							
-3	-2	-1	0	+1	+2	+3				

Mood right now

Energy level right now

Feeling of mastery or control over _____ (highest since this time yesterday)

General feelings of depression (greatest since this time yesterday)

Feelings of self-satisfaction
1. Highest since this time yesterday
2. What was happening?
3. Lowest since this time yesterday
4. What was happening?

Figure 12.1b *Data gathering format for use at outset of each session (side b).*

Name :_____ Date :_____

Therapist Name :_____ SS # :_____

Best Experience
Fill out each day after supper and before bedtime

	Date	Time Period	Situation	Rating: See Below
1.				
2.				
3.				
4.				
5.				
6.				
7.				
8.				
9.				
10.				
11.				
12.				

Scale:
+5 (as good an experience as I can ever imagine);+4;+3;+2;+1(just noticeably good);
0 (neutral);
-1 (just noticeably bad);-2;-3;-4;-5 (as bad an experience as I can ever imagine).

Figure 12.2. *Record-keeping format for daily use.*

(1) The most powerful stress-or anger-producing experience
     of the day
(2) The worst experience of the day
(3) The best experience of the day

I decide on which of these to request on the basis of an
assortment of hunches – and I usually select item (3). The format
for this assignment is shown in Figure 12.2. The scales shown in
this figure require some comment. When I first began using this
assignment, I found that some clients were avoiding record keeping
with the excuse "I didn't have any good experiences, so I didn't
have anything to keep a record of." Because I want each client to
keep a record of something each day, I changed the scale. Now I
say, "If you don't have any good experiences, just fill in your least
lousy experience of the day. That way you will have something to
record each day." These records and the behavioral interview are
used to select stressful and anger-producing stimuli for use in the
third phase of treatment.

Phase II

Phase II entails at least three one-hour sessions for practicing
relaxation and biofeedback. The client first learns a simple
relaxation technique based on the procedure of Benson et al.,
(1974). The technique takes about 20 minutes, and the client is
asked to practice it once a day for the duration of treatment. The
client then learns to lower sympathetic tone using relaxation and
biofeedback (with a continuous analog tone). At the end of the
second phase, the client is taught a rapid relaxation strategy (similar
to that of Stroebel, 1982) using the following instructions:

> Focus on your breathing – take a deeper than normal
> breath and breathe out through your nose – on the
> out breath think the word "calm" and smile to
> yourself. Let a warm comfortable sensation develop
> in your hands and stomach. Do it again. Each
> breath takes about 10 seconds; the whole exercise
> takes about 20 seconds. At the end of this quick
> calming response notice how much better you feel.
> Try to do this at least 12 times per day. (Some
> people have reminded themselves to practice this
> response by doing it each time they look at a watch

or a clock, each time they enter a bathroom, and each
time they hear a phone ring.)

The first two phases are usually completed within four to five
sessions.

Phase III

Phase III incudes an average of 13 one-hour treatment sessions
as well as daily homework (record-keeping assignments and
relaxation practice, aided for many clients by a portable biofeedback
unit). During the treatment sessions, two-minute, semistructured
"stress interviews" (Almy, 1978) alternate with five-minute
relaxation periods. As mentioned above, the stressful material for
the two-minute interview is based on previously gathered (and
continuously updated) information about stress-or anger-producing
situations appropriate for the particular client. During the first few
stress interview periods the client is instructed, "Let yourself feel
and express anger (or upset), without becoming physically violent."
During the first few sessions the client receives continuous visual
analog biofeedback during several cycles of two-minute stress and
five-minute relaxation periods. The array of equipment shown in
Figure 1.1 of Chapter 1 is often used at this stage. In early
sessions, and at the outset of other sessions, the stress interview
often includes simulation (via role playing) of the stressful or
anger-producing situation. At the end of each two-minute stress
interview, the client is instructed, "Put those things out of your mind
and relax deeply and quickly."

After the first several sessions of this phase, clients are also
taught to alter their cognitive processes (covert verbalizations and
imagery) in response to simulations and descriptions of situations
that would previously have provoked stress or anger. For example,
the violent client is asked to consider anger as a secondary emotion
that rapidly follows a drop in self-esteem, which is accompanied by
an emotion such as humiliation, frustration, or fear; the client is
asked to identify and describe aloud the original emotion (much
individual tailoring is necessary here).

In the later sessions of this phase, the feedback system is
occasionally turned off (i.e., feedback tones and video feedback are
not presented to the client during a cycle of relaxation-stress

interview-relaxation). Following this, we discuss feelings and events that occurred during the cycle. Particular attention is paid to the client's estimation of his or her own stimulus value (i.e., how others might perceive him or her) at various points during the stress interview. We also attend to a violent client's feelings of, perception of, and control over the fire in the boiler, without the aid of simultaneous biofeedback. Following this discussion, the videotape of the cycle is replayed, and the actual relationships of the behavioral and biological variables are observed as they occurred together in real time. At the end of each session, the client is shown a simple graph of the results of at least one cycle of relaxation-stress-relaxation, which is compared with graphs from prior sessions; changes in duration and level of arousal are highlighted.

With most clients, models, mini-models, and a personality theory are developed and discussed during some sessions. After approximately 17 sessions, treatment is terminated and follow-up visits are scheduled; for most violent clients, follow-up continues for several years, with visits scheduled every one to three months.

Results and Discussion

With the sample of 62 violent clients, we have monitored treatment effects on numerous dependent variables (behavioral, physiological, and subjective). The remainder of the chapter will examine the impact of the treatment program in the context of several crucial dependent variables. But first, I will briefly review an important result that directly relates to the client as coinvestigator and personal theorist.

Record Keeping

By the end of formal treatment the data on compliance with record-keeping instructions are very clear. Of the 62 clients I followed most closely, 37 complied with the record-keeping assignments. Of these 37, 30 showed at least an 80 percent reduction in frequency of physically violent episodes, with marked reduction in severity and duration. Improvement was such that police were not involved in subsequent episodes, while police had been involved with many of their episodes prior to the start of treatment. Of the clients who did not comply with record-keeping assignments, only two showed an 80 percent reduction in frequency of physically violent behavior.[1]

Follow-Up

We have recently been able to obtain a detailed follow-up on 25 of these 62 clients, and the results are shown in Table 12.1. These data show that reductions in the severity and frequency of most clients' angry feelings and violent behavior (henceforth collectively referred to as "hostility") have been maintained from six months to ten years since the end of formal treatment. In many of the cases shown in Table 12.1, we have been able to obtain the cooperation of people who know the client well (probation officers, spouses, friends, children) in order to get independent corroboration on such data as the types and frequencies of violent outbursts.

The comparison of the follow-up data (shown in the last column of Table 12.1) with behavioral status at the end of treatment (not shown) indicates a surprising degree of stability. Only one of these 25 clients (#11) is clearly worse since the end of treatment. Coincidentally another client (#12) has improved, to the same extent, since the end of treatment. Among these 25 clients there is a statistically significant point- biserial correlation of record keeping with hostility change (degrees of freedom = 23; t value is 1.18; p<0.05 one-tail) indicating that greater hostility change was shown among those clients who kept records. This comparison provides support for the observation made with the 62 clients described above.

Table 12.1 and its footnotes explain the methods of converting hostility levels and frequencies into numbers. Table 12.2 presents a comparison of the ten clients showing the greatest hostility change

---

[1] The correlation between compliance with record keeping and treatment success is now used as the basis of the following printed policy, which is handed out to each client at the start of treatment: "All clients must keep records during each week of treatment. The second failure to comply with this requirement will result in immediate discharge; at the time of this discharge the client will be given two weeks' worth of blank record-keeping sheets and an envelope addressed to us. If the client decides that he/she would like to get back into treatment, he/she should complete two weeks' worth of record-keeping and return the complete data sheets to us. When we receive these two weeks of complete records, we will put the client at the bottom of our waiting list."

Table 12.1
Individual Data Pre-and Post Treatment for Clients in Follow-Up Sample

| | | | SKIN CONDUCTANCE LEVELS (scaled to range from 0 to 1) | | | |
| | | | Minimums | | Maximums | |
Client	Sessions	Record Keeping?	Pre	Post	Pre	Post
1	15	Y	.18	.10	.30	.10
2	11	Y	.30	.10	.73	1.00
3 (Mr.B)	40+	Y	.60	.20	1.00	.50
4	09	Y	-	-	-	-
5	20	Y	-	-	-	-
6	33	Y	.04	.02	.07	.03
7 (Mr.A)	40+	Y	.65	.40	1.00	.98
8	40+	N	.65	.10	.70	.15
9	10	Y	.16	.46	.25	.58
10 (Mr.D)	40+	Y	.55	.15	.90	.20
11	18	Y	.85	.40	.89	.61
12	21	N	.61	.30	.90	.80
13	19	Y	.71	.80	.90	.86
14	10	N	.87	.62	.92	.81
15	09	N	.30	.58	.59	.70
16	28	Y	.20	.08	.25	.10
17	10	Y	.46	.48	.80	.78
18	15	Y	.23	.09	.26	.15
19	11	Y	.45	.20	.70	.52
20	07	N	-	.10	-	.41
21 (Mr.C)	40+	Y	.55	.25	.71	.36
22	11	N	.06	.04	1.00	.06
23	36	Y	.65	.18	.69	.22
24	10	Y	-	-	-	-
25	18	N	.85	.80	.90	.82
MEANS	20.8		.498	.293	.689	.488
SD	12.2		.246	.241	.291	.324

NOTE: Y=Yes, record keeping was done; N=Not done. (-)=No data for that variable.
   a) 1/2 "life" refers to how long it takes, in minutes, to return 1/2 way to the pre stress level of skin conductance.
   b) Feel no anger = 0,Feel anger = F, Express anger = E, Threaten = T, Grab or push = G, Hit = H. These items were scored using the following numbers:
        O = 1, F= 2, E = 3, T = 4, G = 5, H = 6.
Mean and SD of frequencies are expressed in decimals and presented in parentheses.

Table 12.1   (continued)

Skin Conductance Arousal Duration (1/2 Life in minutes)[a]				Highest Level of Anger or Violent Behavior in prior week [b] (frequency in prior week)	
Stress Profile		Stress Interview			
Pre	Post	Pre	Post	Pre	Post[c]
1.0	1.0	2.0	0.5	H (1)	E (5)
-.-	-.-	-.-	-.-	T (1)	F (2)
4.0	0.5	5.0+	0.5	H (1)	F (1)
-.-	-.-	-.-	-.-	E (7)	0
-.-	-.-	-.-	-.-	H (1)	E (1)
5.0+	2.0	5.0+	3.0	T (1)	E (1)
3.5	1.0	5.0+	0.5	H (2)	F (2)
1.0	0.5	4.0	2.75	H (1)	G (1)
2.0	0.2	5.0+	0.75	H (1)	T (1)
2.5	0.6	5.0+	0.75	H (4)	E (1)
3.25	-.-	3.0	1.25	H (1)	H (1)
5.0+	5.0+	5.0+	2.0	H (1)	E (1)
0.5	0.5	2.25	1.0	E (4)	E (1)
1.5	-.-	0.5	1.5	E (7)	E (1)
3.75	1.5	2.75	0.75	T (1)	0
-.-	1.25	1.25	0.75	E (1)	F (7)
1.25	1.25	5.0+	2.0	T (1)	0
-.-	-.-	0.5	1.5	H (1)	E (3)
5.0+	-.-	0.5	1.0	T (1)	E (1)
-.-	-.-	-.-	5.0+	G (7)	G (4)
5.0+	0.5	5.0+	0.5	H (1)	T (1)
5.0+	-.-	5.0+	-.-	E (3)	E (4)
-.-	-.-	-.-	5.0+	H (4)	E (2)
-.-	-.-	-.-	-.-	E (1)	O
1.0	0.5	2.0	1.0	T (4)	T (1)
4.25	2.24	4.83	2.70	4.76(.232)	2.72(.168)
2.10	1.46	2.28	1.64	1.30(.210)	1.59(.170)

NOTE: c) This measure was taken in a follow-up questionnaire and/or phone conversation (follow-up durations ranged from 6 months to 10 years after the end of formal treatment); all other Post measures were taken at the client's last formal treatment session, or during a follow-up visit.

Table 12.2
*Data for Top vs Bottom Ten Clients-in Terms of Hostility Change from Pre
Treatment to Follow-Up (Some Clients Have Incomplete Data)*

VARIABLES	ALL CLIENTS WITH DATA			TOP TEN CLIENTS		
	MEAN	SD	N	MEAN	SD	N
Sessions	21.75	12.22	20	24.0	13.6	10
Record Keeping	.650	.489	20	.800	.422	10
Skin Conductance Pre Minimum	.55	.24	17	.51	.16	8
Skin Conductance Post Minimum	.31	.26	18	.30	.17	8
Skin Conductance Pre Maximum	.73	.29	17	.77	.25	8
Skin Conductance Post Maximum	.48	.32	18	.54	.32	8
Stress Profile S C Arousal Duration Pre	3.30	2.08	14	3.50	1.59	6
Stress Profile S C Arousal Duration Post	1.42	1.60	11	1.81	2.09	6

Table 12.2 (continued)

| BOTTOM TEN CLIENTS | | | STATISTICAL OBSERVATIONS |
MEAN	SD	N	
19.5	10.9	10	There is no significant correlation between number of sessions and hostility change when all 25 subjects are included.
.500	.527	10	There is a significant point biserial correlation (p<.05, 1 tail) showing that complying with record keeping assignments is related to greater hostility change.
.58	.30	9	The most important feature here is that more successful clients have a higher range of Skin Conductance Level pre treatment; among all 25 men the correlation of hostility change with Skin Conductance range is .43 (p=0.027).
.32	.32	10	
.70	.33	9	
.44	.33	10	
3.16	2.49	8	These numbers are not significantly different.
0.95	.57	5	

Table 12.2 (continued)

VARIABLES	ALL CLIENTS WITH DATA			TOP TEN CLIENTS		
	MEAN	SD	N	MEAN	SD	N
Stress Interview S C Arousal Duration Pre	3.67	2.31	16	4.75	2.23	7
Stress Interview S C Arousal Duration Post	1.90	1.71	17	1.75	1.83	8
Hostility Level (With Frequency Added as a Decimal Value) Pre	4.97	1.24	20	5.53	1.09	10
Hostility Level (With Frequency Added as a Decimal Value) Post	3.12	1.35	20	2.31	0.99	10

NOTE: Statistical observations are based on correlational analyses, analyses of variance and analyses of covariance for all variables except the record keeping. Record keeping was evaluated using point biserial correlational analyses. All p values were 2-tail unless otherwise noted.

Table 12.2 (continued)

| BOTTOM TEN CLIENTS | | | STATISTICAL OBSERVATIONS |
MEAN	SD	N	
2.83	2.12	9	In all 25 clients there is a significant correlation ($r=.61$, $p=0.003$) between interview duration decreases and hostility change. ANOVA shows the top 10 men have greatest interview decrease ($p<.02$), but ANCOVA shows
2.03	1.69	9	that when the difference in pre treatment duration is covaried out there is no remaining difference in duration change.
4.40	1.16	10	These numbers represent a significant difference between pre treatment levels and a persisting significant difference in change scores when the pre treatment differences are covaried out ($p<.001$).
3.92	1.19	10	

Table 12.3
Data for Top vs Bottom Six Clients-in Terms of Hostility Change from Pre Treatment to Follow-Up (All Clients Have Complete Data)

VARIABLES	ALL TWELVE CLIENTS		TOP SIX CLIENTS	
	MEAN	SD	MEAN	SD
Sessions	26.67	13.26	26.67	15.20
Record Keeping	Four of the top six and four of the bottom 6 clients kept records; however, in all 25 clients record keeping was found to be related to hostility change. (See Figure 12.2)			
Skin Conductance Pre Minimum	.51	.23	.53	.13
Skin Conductance Post Minimum	.38	.26	.35	.17
Skin Conductance Pre Maximum	.73	.29	.87	.15
Skin Conductance Post Maximum	.56	.31	.66	.27
Stress Profile S C Arousal Duration Pre	3.13	2.07	3.50	1.59
Stress Profile S C Arousal Duration Post	1.25	1.58	1.81	2.09

NOTE: Statistical observations are based on correlational analyses, analyses of variance and analyses of covariance for all variables   except the record keeping. Record keeping was evaluated using point biserial correlational analyses. All p values were 2-tail unless otherwise noted

Table 12.3 (continued)

| BOTTOM SIX CLIENTS | | STATISTICAL OBSERVATIONS |
MEAN	SD	
26.67	12.71	These numbers are not significantly different.
.49	.32	
.41	.34	
.59	.35	
.47	.35	
2.75	2.56	The pre treatment duration is related to change in duration (F is significant at .02), but significant differences do not show up in change scores when the pre treatment differences are statistically controlled.
0.70	.65	

Table 12.3 (continued)

VARIABLES	ALL TWELVE CLIENTS		TOP SIX CLIENTS	
	MEAN	SD	MEAN	SD
Stress Interview S C Arousal Duration Pre	4.92	1.67	5.46	1.33
Stress Interview S C Arousal Duration Post	1.29	.90	1.08	.71
Hostility Level (With Frequency Added as a Decimal Value) Pre	5.27	1.13	5.50	1.09
Hostility Level (With Frequency Added as a Decimal Value) Post	3.01	1.26	2.08	0.94

Table 12.3 (continued)

| BOTTOM SIX CLIENTS | | STATISTICAL OBSERVATIONS |
MEAN	SD	
4.38	1.91	The pre score is related to change score (F is significant beyond .001) but significant differences do not show up in change scores when the pretreatment differences are statistically controlled. There is also a significant correlation
1.50	1.08	$(r=.59, p=.02)$ between change in duration of arousal during stress interview and change in hostility.
5.03	1.21	These numbers represent a significant difference between pre treatment levels and a persisting significant difference in change scores when the pre treatment differences are covaried out $(p<.001)$.
3.93	.75	

with the ten clients showing the least hostility change. We have complete data for only 13 of these clients, and the top and bottom six (in terms of hostility change) are separately presented in Table 12.3. The statistical analysis strategies are specified in the footnote of Table 12.2.

The hostility differences between the top and bottom groups show up clearly in analyses of covariance. These differences are clear in both the evaluation of groups of ten (Table 12.2) and groups of six (Table 12.3). The results indicate that those clients who show the most change in hostility also show greater hostility levels prior to treatment, and when this difference is covaried out they continue to show highly significant differences in hostility change. In other words, although the level and frequency of hostility at the outset of treatment is related to change in hostility over the course of treatment, the statistical analyses indicate that improvements occurred which are not merely due to the pre-treatment hostility level. Therefore the changes observed can not be explained merely by "regression to the mean."

Examination of the relationship between number of sessions and amount of hostility change shows no significant relationship when the 25 clients are taken together. Furthermore there is no significant difference when the top ten and bottom ten clients are compared. However, it is worth noting that in some parts of our sample we can see a correlation between sessions and degree of hostility change. (For example among the top six men of the 13 for whom we have complete data, a higher number of sessions correlates with a greater degree of hostility change, p=.02.) A higher number of sessions also correlates with some other variables; the most statistically significant of these correlations shows that the higher number of sessions correlates with higher levels of pretreatment hostility (p=.006).

Physiological Data

Four different generations of skin-conductance detection systems were used between 1974 and the present (different apparatus, electrode type and size, and gel). While these changes do not appear to influence the duration of the arousal response, they do alter the absolute values. In order to deal with these differences in detection systems, I have related each minimum and maximum value obtained for a violent client using a particular detection system to the total range obtained with that system for all clients (violent and nonviolent). I used the transformation method described by Cohen et al., (1978) and by Berman and Johnson (1985) for obtaining range-corrected standardized scores. The range extends from 0 to 1. For example, with a client whose minimum value is halfway up the range obtained with that particular detection system, the transformation would result in a .5 being given as the minimum value for this client. Use of these transformations permits us to examine a variety of relationships.

Perusal of the Tables indicates that there is a reduction in skin-conductance values (both maximum and minimum), and a reduction in durations of skin conductance arousal in both the stress profile and the stress interview.

Among the skin conductance minimum and maximum measures there is one difference that stands out as being particularly robust, indicating that a higher range of skin conductance pretreatment is characteristic of those clients who will show greater hostility change. Note that these same clients also show a higher range of skin-conductance after treatment, but that the maximum and minimum values are lower at the end of treatment (the change scores are also significant in some of the comparisons).

Turning to the duration measures, we see that the durations of skin conductance arousal in the stress-profile evaluation do not show a clear relationship with overall hostility change, even though some subsets of the data show statistically significant relationships. One of the largest is a relationship between change (pre-to posttreatment) in duration of arousal in the stress profile and change in duration of arousal in the stress interview ($r=.566$; $p=.02$).

Initially I was surprised to see that the stress profile did not show greater relationship to other variables. However, later reflection reminded me of my own observations, as well as published observations, which indicate that stressors selected for each individual client are more likely to show diagnostic effects than are standardized stressors (e.g., Flor, Turk, and Birbaumer, 1985). Accordingly, the individualized stress interviews do show much greater relationship between the duration variables and hostility change than is shown between the standardized stress profile and hostility change.

The one variable which shows the most clear relationship with hostility change (showing up in the analysis of variance and in all correlations) is the arousal duration during the pretreatment[2] stress interview (all p values are beyond the .02 level with 2-tailed tests). As indicated in the statistical observations section of Table 12.2, the analysis of covariance shows that the change in interview duration is not significantly different between the top and bottom ten men when the large differences in duration of the pretreatment stress interview are covaried out. However, in other comparisons (with all 25 men and with the 13 men for whom we have complete data) we find a strong relationship between duration of arousal in the stress interview and hostility change. The clients who show the greatest hostility change also show lower durations of arousal following the stress interview at the end of treatment, as well as the expected difference in degree of change in duration of stress interview arousal between pre-and posttreatment.

These relationships suggest that it may be possible to predict which clients will do well (in terms of decrease in hostility as a result of treatment) by attending to a combination of variables that can be measured at the outset of treatment.[3]

In fact, in the sample of only 13 clients for whom we have complete data, a multiple regresssion analysis shows that the combination of range of skin conductance prior to treatment and level of hostility prior to treatment predicts change in hostility, accounting for over 60 percent of the variance ($r=.78$; $r^2=.61$).

Possible Explanations

An attempt to explain these behavioral and biological observations brings to mind the issues of habituation, placebo effects, and skill acquisition. From another study we have some data that pertain to the habituation and skill-acquisition issues: we found no signs of habituation to the stress profile when ten normal subjects were tested twice (using alternative forms of the quiz), with at least 34 hours separating the two experimental sessions. On the placebo issue, we have subjective reports from some individuals who failed to show

[2] This is a liberal use of the word "pretreatment:" the first stress interview is conducted in the fifth or sixth session, when some treatment has actually started.

[3] As mentioned earlier, the compliance with record-keeping instructions is an excellent predictor; after a few sessions it becomes obvious which clients are going to comply with these instructions.

reductions in the recovery time for autonomic function, and nevertheless report that they have developed some mastery over their emotional arousal as a result of the treatment sequence. The data on the ten normal subjects argue for a skill-acquisition explanation of these results, while the data on those who showed no reduction in duration of   autonomic arousal argue for the possibility of a placebo effect.

Between these two extremes are many points at which habituation has probably played a large role. For example, it seems likely that some habituation may have occurred as a result of repeated exposure to stress interviews between the first and second exposures to the standardized stressors.   Even the least successful clients, in terms of reduction of violent behavior, showed shorter autonomic half-lives in response to both the stress interview and the stress profile at the end of treatment. Note again that the stress material is constantly updated and that the amplitude of response to a stress- interview stimulus item that produced a large response at the end of treatment was almost the same as that observed at the beginning of treatment. By the end of treatment, the number of stimuli capable of producing an episode of clear autonomic arousal was typically reduced; however, we were usually able to identify at least one arousal-provoking stimulus for each session.

As I look back on all of my experience with this general strategy, I conclude that habituation, skill acquisition, and placebo effects probably all play important roles in the success of treatment. The simple exercise of considering troublesome stimuli – as well as alternative responses to these stimuli – in a relatively safe situation, with no behavioral outbursts occurring, seems likely to have had a variety of effects. Further work will be necessary if we are to clarify the approximate contributions of placebo effects and such factors as habituation, skill acquisition, response prevention, and changes in expectancy and disposition, as well as changes in the working self-concept. However, it is my guess that very little resolution or generalization will be possible from client to client about the contribution of these various factors because of the wide individual differences.

To illustrate and perhaps to help resolve the role of these individual differences, the next chapter presents the details of treatment features and results for four individuals.

13 : Case Histories and Treatment Details[1]

Here I hope to show how all the concepts and strategies discussed up to this point can be put together to help some of the most stressed and stressful people I have ever known. The chapter is divided into five sections. In each of the first four sections I will present an individual member of our sample of violent clients. In the course of these presentations, I will describe how we used the assessment and treatment methods outlined in Chapter 12, and the results for each individual. In the fifth and final section, you will read about some adaptations in procedure for three clients who could not profit from the strategies described in Chapter 12.

Mr. A

Mr. A, a 47-year-old man, showed more frequent and severe violent behavior than most of our clients. His status at the time of our initial assessment is shown in Figure 13.1. He had an eighth-grade education and normal intelligence. He is five feet, ten inches tall, and at the beginning of treatment he weighed 210 pounds. He was an illegitimate child and had spent some of his early years in foster homes. In Mr. A's early years he was repeatedly abused by foster parents and older neighbors. He became suspicious and uncooperative. This probably accounts for his obtaining a low score on a childhood IQ test and eventually being placed in an institution for retarded children for several months. He also spent some time in reform school, and when I first met him, in

[1] Informed consent was obtained from all clients and demographic details have been altered to protect anonymity.

1980, he had been in prison for assault, or in mental hospitals, at least once each year since he was 15 years old.

He recalls an episode when he was 11 years old during which he was being tormented by two older and larger boys. He broke free and was able to seriously injure one of the boys; the other boy left Mr. A alone (this episode is depicted in Figure 13.2). From this episode Mr. A got the reputation of being a very dangerous (hostile) person who would hurt others if he got a chance. Even when he was overpowered, he would not give in or cease trying to hurt other people. Mr. A perceives this as a very important time in the development of his reputation – a reputation that he said "saved me from a lot of hassles – because the other guys knew I didn't fool around." This appears to have been the pivotal episode of negative reinforcement in Mr. A's early life. In each new situation of a move to a new neighborhood or a new institution, Mr. A had to reestablish his reputation – and thus experienced further episodes of negative reinforcement that further strengthened his tendency to quickly become violent when he was upset.

At 16-and-a-half years of age, Mr. A took an assumed name and lied about his age to enlist in the military. He was in combat in Korea and Vietnam (taking a second assumed name to get into the service during the Vietnam era). His military record was spotty, with excellent ratings in some activities but with evidence of great difficulty in dealing with authority figures; this resulted in his spending much time in the brig. After his discharge from the service, he continued to have trouble with the law, and, in fact, other than his time in the military, his longest single period out of jail or a mental institution from age 15 to age 47 was about three months. He was once convicted of manslaughter, and at one point he spent 12 consecutive years in prison. He reported that he spent most of his prison time in solitary confinement because of his violent behavior. Prior to treatment with us, Mr. A had been extensively treated with psychotherapy, electroconvulsive shock therapy, and medication (including 16 months of lithium) for a variety of problems – bipolar disorder, paranoia, impulsive behavior problems, and outbursts of rage. A neurological exam, with EEG, showed results within normal limits. Prior to treatment, Mr. A's violent behavior patterns included threats and shoving on the average of more than twice a week. If his antagonist showed any resistance, Mr. A immediately escalated to hitting until he or his antagonist lost consciousness, or until Mr. A was firmly restrained. Attempts to restrain Mr. A generally required more than one individual, and usually resulted in injury to several people because of Mr. A's considerable strength and general physical fitness (he has been doing calisthenics, lifting weights, and running for years).

At the time of assessment Mr. A was very agitated and emotionally labile, and he talked loudly. He did not seem to listen to or respond to anything except for direct commands and questions. These problems became much less severe during the first few relaxation and biofeedback sessions. During the first six sessions of treatment, Mr. A's violent behavior also decreased rapidly, and at no time since the beginning of treatment has he spent a night in jail – in marked contrast to his pretreatment jail record. Since the beginning of treatment, he has been directly involved with the police only one time, and this was between the third and fourth sessions. The duration of his autonomic arousal after the standardized stress profiles and the stress interviews has decreased (see Figures 13.3 and 13.4). While there was only a slight decrease in the amplitude of arousal during the stress interviews, Mr. A explained that he could now detect in himself the early signs of increasing arousal without the use of biofeedback. Duration of arousal outside the therapy sessions was also dramatically reduced. Prior to treatment, Mr. A became angry frequently enough, and stayed angry long enough, so that he reported being angry "most of the time." Prior to treatment, he would usually express anger and threaten or hit other people about twice each week. The angry feelings stayed with him for about two days. After the sixth treatment session, these episodes of expression of anger were much more mild – involving less explicit threats and with angry feelings lasting for only hours (rather than days). By this time, the frequency of his expressions of anger was reduced to about once per week.

Mr. A lived far from the hospital and obtained a full-time job shortly after we began working with him. Because of this, we were not able to schedule sessions as close together as we would have preferred. In the ninth month of treatment (after 12 sessions), Mr. A described a wave of calm that came over him while he held the shirt of a man whose dog had bitten him. Mr. A released the man and dealt with the situation in a reasonably calm manner. (He attributed this wave of calm to the biofeedback training and claimed that he had visualized the therapy room and biofeedback apparatus.) Shortly after this episode, we gradually decreased the frequency of Mr. A's visits from once monthly to once every three months to maintain his coping skills and to allow follow-up. The follow-up program with Mr. A (and many other clients) included occasional record-keeping assignments and reminders about continuing practice of strategies he had learned. The following paragraph is the text of a letter I sent to Mr. A in late 1982.

September 20, 1982

Dear Mr. A:

We recently received your record keeping - we only saw three dates entered on it. The idea is to use this thing *every day*.

Please use the enclosed form *every day*. Fill it out between suppertime and bedtime each day. Describe the *most successful* use of the quick calming response during that day.

You should be using this quick calming response at least twelve times each day – as directed on the back of the record-keeping sheet. Use it every time you hear a phone ring, use it every time you go to the bathroom, use it every time you look at your watch. This should add up to about twelve times per day.

When you have completed a week of this record keeping, please mail it back to us in the envelope we have provided.

Sincerely,

John A. Corson, Ph.D.
Psychology, Veterans Administration Hospital

enclosures

In the most recent five years, Mr. A has been physically violent twice, but he has stopped himself short of inflicting any serious physical injury; one episode of violence occurred in a restaurant in response to an insult from an old antagonist, and the other occurred during an episode when Mr. A's automobile was vandalized. Mr. A reports that his feelings of persecution (which were a constant preoccupation prior to treatment) have decreased "a little," and that his ability to predict and control feelings of anger has increased "a lot."

Mr. A, like several other clients, noticed changes in his energy and eating behaviors since treatment. Mr. A's childhood experiences apparently gave rise to self-doubt, profound insecurity, anger, and the general strategy of "always be on guard" and "get them before they get you." This strategy suggests that chronically high resting levels of sympathetic activity were accompanied by a high degree of sympathetic reactivity. This pattern was confirmed in the initial psychophysiological assessments. This chronically high arousal seemed to affect both eating behaviors and energy levels. Mr. A described bouts of overeating and periods of intense fatigue prior to the onset of treatment. He now weighs 175 pounds (down from 210) and reports that he is able to eat normally and that he very rarely feels fatigued. He also reports that his sleep patterns and his ability to concentrate have improved since treatment, and he describes a dramatic reduction in his subjective feelings of muscle tension and general agitation. He is now fully employed and returns for follow-up sessions once every three months. His current status is depicted in Figure 13.5.

Name Mr. A (Pretreatment)   Education 8th Grade (GED?)   Marital Status Divorce x2 Referred by Dr. P

Date 12/20/80   Age 45   Occupation Laborer   Presenting Problems Violent Behavior,

etc.

STIMULI	PRESUMED INTERNAL PROCESSES	TARGET PROBLEMS	TREATMENT METHODS	EVALUATION METHODS
Authority Figures "Police" "Local Politicians" "Injustices"	Fear? Humiliation? → "Anger" Self-esteem drops SELF-CONCEPT: "Hair trigger"; "I get even"; "Outsider"; "Paranoid about some things"; "I'm always ready"; "I get them before they get me"; "I'm a hard worker"; "Hostile"; "I've got a reputation".	Violent Behavior Many fist fights; Shoves, threats; Many arrests; One manslaughter conviction.	Relaxation, Biofeedback, Anger management training (stress interview/role playing interpolated between periods of relaxation and biofeedback throughout), Social skills training, assertion training.	Record keeping best and worst experiences. Psychophysiological monitoring: SCL= .65 to 1.0, BP = 147/97. #Arrests, #Days in jail, #Fights (at outset hit twice last week). Paranoid scale = Hi; Anger/violence scale= Hi;
Life History of abuse, isolation and violence. Foster homes; Reform School; Institution for retarded people;	Hoped for Possible Selves: Respected, Dominant	Substance Abuse History of ETOH, Heroin and other drugs (not for the last 5 years). Depression Made a suicide attempt at age 14.	Is now on BP meds-has been for 2 years. Prior treatments:	WAIS V = 94, P = 99, FS = 96;

State Hospital; Jails and prisons. Combat Experience Korea and Vietnam Memory of getting a "reputation" by fighting.	Feared Possible Selves: Victim Chronic high arousal and high reactivity.	Social Behavior : Talks loudly, Doesn't listen; Emotional lability (laughed loudly 2x and cried 3x during initial interview); Litigious, takes offense easily. Hypertension	Was in state hospital and had ECT before age 20; At various times was on Lithium, Haldol, Librium and other medications. Had 2 1/2 years "off and on" Psychotherapy - ended 1 year ago. Hopes, Interests, Hobbies: A better job, more pay, Interested in dogs, cares for dogs, lifts weights, "works out."	Wechsler Memory = 82; Halstead-Reitan index =.7 (suggests possible diffuse bilateral impairment). Zung = 56 (significant depression). Notes: Had psych testing before age 16-IQ=67, was placed in an institute for retarded people for several months, failed 3rd grade in school, longest period out of jail (other than in Military) about 3 months since age 15; longest jail term was 12 years. Neurology work up and EEG normal.

Figure 13.1. *Pretreatment flow diagram for Mr. A.*

Environment
(two other boys age 14)

Patient
at age 11

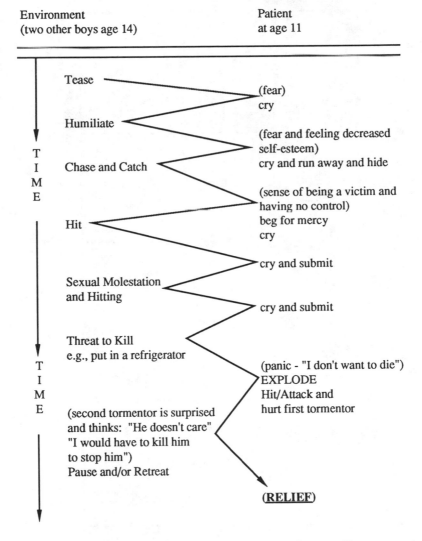

Figure 13.2. *Mr. A's violent episode at age 11.*

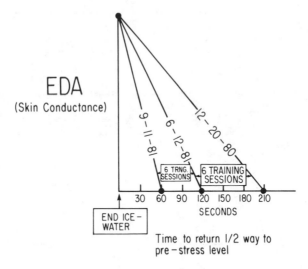

Figure 13.3. *Mr. A's recovery from stress profile is more rapid as training progresses.*

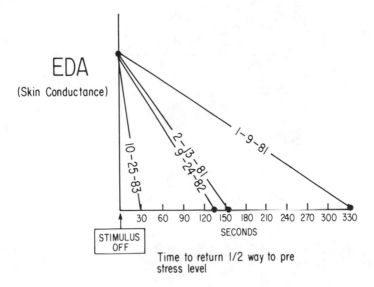

Figure 13.4. *Mr. A's recovery from stress interview is more rapid as training progresses.*

Name Mr. A (Post-treatment) Education 8th Grade (GED?) Marital Status Divorce x2 Referred by Dr. P

Date 1/12/87 Age 52 Occupation Laborer Presenting Problems Violent Behavior,

etc.

STIMULI	PRESUMED INTERNAL PROCESSES	TARGET PROBLEMS	TREATMENT METHODS	EVALUATION METHODS
Same as in 1980 Now the "ordinary hassles" of daily life shift from session to session, e.g., over the last 2 sessions 1) lazy co-worker, 2) woman friend having financial problems.	Self-Concept: "I'm still paranoid, I just don't let it get to me". "I mind my own business". "I'm a hard worker". "I've got a pretty good life now". Hoped for Possible Selves: Respected Feared Possible Selves: Victim Lower resting arousal level and lower reactivity.	Violent Behavior? Reports persisting paranoid feelings and occasional feelings of anger. Substance Abuse? "None since 1975" Depression "Not now" Social Behavior? Listens better, talks more quietly, less	Follow-up once every 3 months; anger management booster sessions.	Assign occasional record keeping (results are uniformly good, compliance is excellent). Psychophysiological monitoring: SCL = .25 - .5 BP = 140/85. #Arrests = 0 in 6 years #Fights = 2 in 5 years (both brief and relatively mild compared to pretreatment).

obvious emotional liability.	Is on same BP meds - same dose as in 1980.		Paranoia Scale = medium to high;
Hypertension ⟶			Anger/Violence Scale = low.
	Hopes, Interests, Hobbies : Is dating "A nice woman", still lifts weights and "works out".		Client's ratings: (on a scale form 0 to 5)
			Sleep-rested? 1980 - 2-3, now - 5.
			Anger 1980 - 5, now - 0-1.
			Anxiety 1980 - 3-4, now - 0.
			Depression 1980 -5, now -0.
			Self Satisfaction 1980 - 2-3, now - 5.

Figure 13.5. *Post-treatment flow diagram for Mr. A.*

Mr. B

Mr. B, a 59-year-old man with some post-high-school education and a verbal IQ of over 130 (Ammons Quick Test), had been taken to police stations more than 50 times by his own count. He had also spent a total of six years in psychiatric hospitals for problems related to assault and episodes of violent behavior. His status at the time of assessement is shown in Figure 13.6. Mr. B is five feet, six inches tall, and he weighed 241 pounds at the start of treatment. The results of Mr. B's neurological exam, with EEG, were within normal limits.

Mr. B was the illegitimate child of a very young woman, and he was brought up as that woman's brother by his grandparents. He was disciplined very harshly as a child, and he cites family tradition as the reason for his harsh treatment. For example, Mr. B was repeatedly locked in a dark closet for long periods of time (at one time for more than 24 hours), and he had all of his fingers broken by a female relative as a punishment for lying. Many pejorative labels were applied to Mr. B during his childhood. Some that had the greatest impact were "bastard," "coward," and "liar". Mr. B was raped by a neighbor and severely beaten by relatives and other neighbors.

When Mr. B was approximately nine years old, he won a fight against three brothers who lived near him (two of these boys were older than Mr. B, and one was bigger and heavier). This victory was after three battles that were watched by Mr. B's father and the father of the brothers. In a situation similar to that described by Mr. A, Mr. B then developed a reputation as one who was not only dangerous and "always ready," but as one who would persist in fighting – he would not give up. Early in Mr. B's teenage years he began to lift weights and started to experience increasing success in fistfights. He eventually acquired a reputation, by his middle and late teenage years, of being a very dangerous person whom no one should "mess with" (he said, "they called me 'lethal' "). Mr. B felt that this reputation helped keep him out of many situations in which he might have been tormented by others; however, he also acknowledges that this reputation probably also got him into many altercations. Again, this early memory represents an episode of very powerful negative reinforcement – with the violent behavior becoming a reliable way of terminating unpleasant experiences.

Mr. B graduated from high school and enlisted in the Army during World War II. He was in combat in Europe and had an excellent record until the war ended, when he quickly got into trouble. He finished his military career in a "neuropsychiatric" hospital.

He is a very articulate man with considerable talent for writing. In an attempt to help us understand the relationship between his early experiences and his violent adult behavior, he has dictated over a dozen tapes and written hundreds of pages over the years since he was first referred to us. From these sources we have been able to construct a detailed history and have developed an understanding of how his working self-concept has evolved through various experiences, and of how he is now able to interact with other people without becoming violent.

Some aspects of Mr. B's medical and behavioral history indicate that some of his episodes of violent behavior may have been due to neurologically based episodic dyscontrol – even though the neurological exam and the scalp EEG showed normal results. Mr. B's descriptions of severe episodes of violent behavior suggest that perhaps one percent of his episodes of violent behavior when he was between 17 and 50 were driven primarily by a neurologically undetected seizure disorder. Evidence in support of this includes Mr. B's description of a strange aura or a sense of impending doom that would occur up to 20 minutes before some of his violent episodes. He also reported having no memory of those violent episodes preceded by an aura – and his first recollection after each of these episodes was waking up, totally restrained, either in jail or in a psychiatric setting. His information about what had happened during these violent episode was gathered from accounts provided by other people. A summary of two such episodes follows.

During an 18-month stay on a locked ward in a psychiatric hospital, Mr. B was walking in a ward hallway near his room when he felt an aura. He recalls reaching out to the wall for a "panic button" that the attendants pushed when they needed help – and this is his last memory prior to awakening in his room totally restrained. He was later told that he began making strange noises and attacking people and eventually had to be restrained by four large men and two women. During the altercation, he inflicted the following injuries: two dislocated shoulders, a broken arm, three broken ribs, a broken nose, and a broken jaw.

When Mr. B was in his early 30s, he recalls driving in a car with his wife and another couple while he was on leave from another mental hospital. It was the Fourth of July and a very warm day. His car was stopped in a line of traffic in a small rural town when the public fireworks display suddenly began. He recalls only a loud noise and a blinding flash (he describes no aura prior to this episode); he later learned that he had left the automobile and begun attacking people. Among the injured were police officers and women and children. His first recollection following this episode is of being totally restrained in the town jail.

When we began treating Mr. B, we noted that his skin conductance rested at a very high level and was also very reactive. My best guess now is that most of Mr. B's violent episodes were triggered by identifiable psychosocial stimuli and were consciously guided throughout and remembered afterwards. But a few episodes, such as those recounted above, were apparently ictal in nature; they seemed to involve a high resting level of autonomic activity, which had the effect of priming or setting levels in damaged central nervous system structures. This sort of episode represents one of three types shown by Mr. B. The second type had a rhythmic temporal quality, and involved going to taverns and slum areas to seek out violent encounters (looking for trouble) at times when he felt the urge to do so.[2] The third type of violent outburst occurred when Mr. B felt that he was "called upon to right some indescribable wrong"; in other words, the third type involved "righteous rage."

The first of these types of violent episodes did not occur during our period of working with Mr. B unless alcohol was involved (though alcohol was not involved in the two episodes recounted above). The second type of episode dropped out by the third month of treatment; prior to that such incidents had been occurring at intervals of once every two to six weeks. The third type did not occur after the 15th session, even though a strong urge to indulge in such behavior can still be triggered by certain experiences (such as observing a man being mean to a woman or child).

We began working with Mr. B in 1981. At that time (and for several years before and after), he was undergoing supportive psychotherapy, which appeared to be of considerable help. Prior to that time he had been extensively treated with ECT, and medication (including lithium for two years) for problems including bipolar disorder, paranoia, and impulsive behavior. None of these treatments appeared to have had much beneficial effect. At the time of beginning treatment with us, he had reduced his drinking to

---

[2] In a recent letter, Mr. B added a postscript saying "I might add: self-induction of mania, together with willful intent, was part of my dysfunction for many, many years."

occasional bouts – once or twice per month. Approximately once per year, a violent episode would occur at the time of alcohol use; one such episode occurred during the early months of treatment, and another occurred during a very stressful period in 1984, when Mr. B was on a follow-up schedule of one visit every three months. Since then he has rarely been intoxicated.

After initial assessment, we conducted 18 weeks of treatment using the format described in Chapter 12 (one session per week). After the sixth session, Mr. B's episodes of violent behavior decreased rapidly from three or more per month to none (unless alcohol was involved) . His feeling of persecution decreased, and his ability to predict and control feelings of anger increased, while the duration of his angry emotions decreased. The duration of his skin-conductance response to the stress profile decreased over the first six training sessions (see Figure 13.7). The duration of his skin conductance responses to the stress interviews also decreased during this period, from over five minutes at the outset to under four minutes. By the 18th treatment session, the duration was usually under two-and-a-half minutes. By the end of treatment, Mr. B's autonomic level (indexed by skin conductance level) was within the normal range in three out of four sessions, while it had been above the normal range for the first eight sessions. At the end of the initial 18 treatment sessions, the frequency of Mr. B's visits was reduced to one per month, for assistance in maintaining his coping skills and to allow for follow-up. After 14 months on this schedule, he was seen once every three months, except for during two highly stressful periods that are described below. Since the initial 18 sessions he has not grabbed or struck another person. On one occasion in 1982, after drinking a large amount of rum, he damaged some property.

As was the case with Mr. A, Mr. B noted that he did not any longer have the uncontrollable urge to overeat. His weight had dropped from 241 to 189 by the end of the 18 weeks of initial treatment and has fluctuated between 180 and 210 since then. Mr. B reports that his sleep pattern and his ability to concentrate have improved since the initial period of treatment, and he describes a dramatic reduction in the subjective feelings of muscle tension and agitation. He even goes as far as to say he now feels serene. He also says that the biofeedback helped him "learn more about the forces within me" and "tune myself to the right level when things get tough."

The first of the two highly stressful situations that occurred after the beginning of Mr. B's treatment concerned pain, immobility, and "hassles" with the medical profession regarding his degenerative arthritis. It has been recommended that he have bilateral knee replacements, and he has been judged to be totally disabled by the Veterans Administration. While he has some trouble walking, he is able to block out pain and do heavy physical labor for short periods of time, even though his physicians have urged him to refrain from this. Over the past two years, he has abided by his physicians' suggestions regarding physical activity, and he is now doing quite well, while still postponing the knee replacements. The most intense upset over his arthritic condition occurred during a period of approximately 18 months, starting in late 1982, when he experienced steadily increasing pain and difficulty in walking. The initial diagnosis was couched in psychiatric terms, and the primary medical aspects of his condition were not acknowledged, until he had become seriously incapacitated. His anger and paranoia (some of which may have been justified) regarding these issues led to many urges to do violence; however, he never acted upon these urges.

The second, and more recent, highly stressful episode occurred when his fifth wife became attached to another man and began spending much time with him. Again, urges to do violence were frequent, but Mr. B had no behavioral outbursts. It is important to note that while Mr. B's arthritic condition is indeed severe, it does not influence the mobility or strength of his upper body. Mr. B could still be readily mistaken for a professional wrestler – in other words, he is still capable of hurting other people if he gives in to the urge to be violent. His post treatment status is shown in Figure 13.8.

In several recent written summaries of his present thoughts regarding his status and history, Mr. B has expressed the idea that he was chronically afraid and felt ugly and deficient – thus he "had something to prove." His account strongly suggests that the cognitive behavior therapy, and the supportive psychotherapy, have helped him develop a general working self-concept, with accompanying attitudes and expectations toward himself and others, that make his life much more pleasant.

While his accounts of earlier episodes of violent behavior – of the second and third types listed above – include internal dialogue, the episodes of dialogue were clearly in service of very simple expectations and dispositions. Now, however, his internal dialogue is much richer and allows him to consider of a variety of behavioral alternatives. Mr. B indicates that before beginning the biofeedback he often felt controlled or driven by bodily forces that he could not understand. After the first 18 sessions of biofeedback, he reported the he could "now pause and question my initial urge – I can talk it over with myself before taking rash action." In fact it now seems that many of the gains made by Mr. B have been directly relatable to his ability to take on the "personal theorist" frame of mind. He has repeatedly told me that the scientist/theorist attitude and the modelling activities give him a feeling of control and understanding, both of which are very important to him.

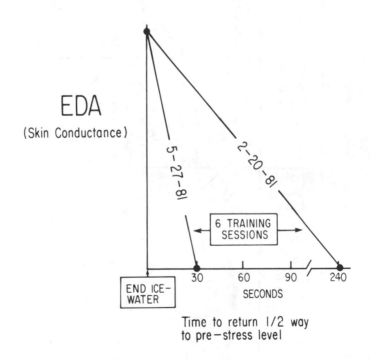

Figure 13.7. *Mr. B's recovery from stress profile is more rapid as training progresses.*

Name Mr. B (pretreatment)   Education some College   Marital Status M 5th wife Referred by Dr. F.

High School,

Date 2/13/81   Age 59   Occupation Skilled Labor/Technician   Presenting Problems Violent behavior

5'6"; 241 lbs

STIMULI	PRESUMED INTERNAL PROCESSES	TARGET PROBLEMS	TREATMENT METHODS	EVALUATION METHODS
Social Situations Social slights	Fear? Humiliation? Self-Esteem drops "Anger"	Violent Behavior Many brawls, fights, threats; many arrests (some violent outbursts may have been seizure related).	Relaxation, Biofeedback, anger management training (stress interview/ role-playing interpolated between periods of relaxation with biofeedback throughout).	Record keeping - best and worst experiences each day. Psychophysiological monitoring: skin conductance level = .6 to 1.0. Weight = 241. #Arrests = none in the last year, #days in jail = none in 1 1/2 years, #expressions of anger = 5 per week, #threats = 3 per week,
Hot weather sudden noises, explosions	Self-Concept: "Lethal"; "Always ready"; "I love a good fight"; "I hit until someone drops"; "You might say I overdo everything."	Substance Abuse History of alcohol "Now only about once every two weeks".	Psychotherapy with Dr. F (Has been going for 2+ years)	
Life history of abuse and violence. Multiple admissions to psychiatric hospitals; multiple (over 50) arrests.	Hoped for Possible Selves: Dominant, Respected, In control.	Overwieght		

Memories of being called "bastard"; "coward"; and "liar"; of being locked in closet for many hours (once for more than 24 hours); of fingers being broken for lying; of being raped; of getting torment to end by fighting.

Feared Possible Selves:
Victim, Humiliated, Incompetent, Controlled.

Chronic high arousal and high reactivity.

Bipolar
(now refuses Lithium)

Prior Treatments:
Psychiatric hospitalizations (in for a total of six years; 18 months on a locked ward). ECT, various meds including Lithium for two years.

Psychotherapy - sporadic with therapists other than Dr. F.

Hopes, Hobbies, Interests:
A better job, interested in dogs, gunsmithing, drawing, carpentry.

#grab, shove = 4 per month,
#hit = 1 time in last week,
#hit to unconcious = last time was two years ago.

Paranoia scale = high;
Anger/violence scale = high.

IQ (Ammons Quick Test) = 130+.

Notes:
Is very articulate writer and draws very well. Neurological work-up/EEG normal.

Figure 13.6. *Pretreatment flow diagram for Mr. B.*

Name Mr. B (post-treatment) Education HS, some College Marital Status Divorced Referred by Dr. F.

Date 2/20/87 Age 65 Occupation Part-time clerk Presenting Problems Violent behavior,

5'6"; 180 lbs

STIMULI	PRESUMED INTERNAL PROCESSES	TARGET PROBLEMS	TREATMENT METHODS	EVALUATION METHODS
Life history and memories - see Pre- treatment flow diagram	Self-Concept: "In control," "serene," "lonely".	Violent Behavior? no violent behavior in several years.	Follow-up occasional visits and monthly contact by mail.	Record keeping - best and worst experiences each day.
	Hoped for Possible Selves: competent, respected, loved, in control.	Substance Abuse? None for over a year.	Hopes, Interests Hobbies: Started working again, hopes to make new	Psychophysiological monitoring: skin conductance level = .2 to .5.
Financial Problems (paying alimony)	Feared Possible Selves: old, lonely, crippled, incompetent, controlled, victim.	Overweight? not currently a problem.	friends, would like to have a woman friend, no longer raises dogs,	Weight = 180.
	Lower resting arousal level and lower reactivity	Bipolar still notes some tendency to highs and	no longer does gun- smithing or carpentry.	No arrests, violence or threats; occasional feelings of anger.

Paranoia scale = low;
Anger/violence scale = low.

Notes:
Is lonely and often sad.

lows, but is able to control them.

Degenerative Arthritis pain, difficulty moving (takes no medication).

Figure 13.8. *Post-treatment flow diagram for Mr. B.*

Mr. C

Mr. C, a 34-year-old man with a college education and a verbal IQ of over 130 (Ammons Quick Test), had been convicted of manslaughter. He had spent several years in prison and many months in psychiatric hospitals for problems related to assault and episodes of violent behavior, as well as for other problems related to depression, substance abuse, and posttraumatic stress disorder. He is five feet, nine inches tall, and at the beginning of treatment he weighed 145 pounds. Neurological examination, with EEG, showed results within normal limits. His status at the time of assessment is shown in Figure 13.9. Mr. C is the youngest of two children born to a career military officer; both parents were alcoholics. In his early years, his family moved frequently, and Mr. C promptly developed a reputation in each new neighborhood and school for being very quick with his fists, short tempered, and dangerous. Mr. C's brother often engineered situations so that Mr. C would feel compelled to get into a fight with someone. Mr. C studied a variety of martial arts and was very careful to keep himself physically fit (except for times when he was abusing drugs or alcohol – at these times he generally avoided situations in which he might feel compelled to fight). With Mr. C, fights took many forms – some being fistfights, others involving knives, and some involving guns. Mr. C reports that he first killed a person, in self-defense, at the age of 15. The incident involved three other people and was a fundamentally racial matter. Mr. C had never seen his victim before, and he is not completely sure that it was as a result of the wounds he inflicted that the victim died. Mr. C was not prosecuted for this assault.

Parts of Mr. C's childhood experience are described in earlier chapters; he was abused physically and psychologically by his father and psychologically by his mother. At one point, one of his fingers was almost totally amputated during a beating by his father, and his older brother had several teeth broken by his father during a period of abuse. When Mr. C was 11-years-old, his father was beating his mother and Mr. C made him stop by threatening him with a pistol. While pointing the pistol at his father and watching his father beg for mercy, Mr. C decided that "from now on I will be the terrorist." This particular episode appears to be the pivotal episode of negative reinforcement in Mr. C's developmental period.

Mr. C enlisted in the military and had a tour of combat duty in Vietnam. Mr. C was briefly a prisoner of war (he escaped) and was brought up on charges twice (once for killing a civilian and once for assaulting an officer). Both charges were dropped. During his time as a prisoner of war, Mr. C was tortured and raped by his captors. He was also severely wounded in his arms and legs in combat in Vietnam. Mr. C now carries a diagnosis of posttraumatic stress disorder and is considered totally disabled.

At the time of Mr. C's referral to us, he was indulging in a wide range of violent acts. These acts included threats to the lives of others (for example, he would talk about explicit details regarding the type of high-powered rifle, explosive, or poison he intended to use) and the occasional severe beatings he administered to other people. Mr. C carried a knife, and frequently a gun. The most severe physical assault he was involved in that we know of since we first assessed him was a pistol whipping (hitting with the butt of a handgun) that he administered to his former wife, rendering her unconcious. During this period, he was making threats of physical violence on an average of twice each week and was involved in public fistfights once every one to three weeks. In the previous 12 months, he had rendered at least two people unconscious. After 20 sessions with very little progress, Mr. C left treatment when we asked him to reduce his use of marijuana (he was smoking from one to three times each day). Mr. C has resumed treatment twice since that time, and only in the most recent sessions has he made progress. He has now reduced his use of marijuana to less than once a week, he has developed skill in controlling autonomic arousal, and he now shows a lower resting level and more rapid recovery from episodes of high autonomic arousal (see Figure 13.10). He has also shown a dramatic reduction in both threatened and actual violence. Mr. C has now been seen by my colleagues and me for over 40 sessions. The last 20 sessions were conducted by me. The first 12 of the most recent 20 sessions were conducted weekly or biweekly, and when progress was noted, the frequency was reduced to once every two to four weeks. Figure 13.11 shows Mr. C's current status and his remaining problems.

Additional understanding of Mr. C's present status, coping strategies, and remaining problems can be gathered from looking at Figures 13.12, 13.13, and 13.14. These three figures depict three points of view on the same episode. Mr. C was having financial problems, his wife was sick, and his daughter was in jail; in short, he was in deep trouble. His first impulses are shown on these various diagrams. While he was in a session with me, I drew these with his input. At the end of the session, I photocopied these figures and gave them to him to take along and think about. When he came back the next week, we discussed the figures again and the fact that he had been able to come to a peaceful solution of the problems that were bothering him during the previous week. He asked me to write "solved" across these diagrams. Close examination of these figures, particularly Figure 13.13, shows the relationships among the fire in the boiler, the working self-concept and the feared possible selves. Making this explicit in a session with a client, such as I did with Mr. C, often seems to be of great help. The impact may be in part akin to a sort of desensitization to the worst possible outcome; this desensitization may allow the client to indulge in a fruitful internal dialogue, which in turn allows more effective problem solving than had been previously possible.

Another way of examining the relationship between the feared possible self and the working self-concept is to pay careful attention to the client's responses to the last two questions shown on the form depicted in Figure 1 of Chapter 12 – specifically, What is the lowest level of self- satisfaction in the last 24 hours, and what was the situation in which this lowest level occurred? The client's responses to these questions (asked at the start of each treatment session) can serve as a guide to a discussion or the development of a model that will help put his worst fears into perspective, and may help facilitate problem solving and improve outcomes.

The primary gains from our work with Mr. C appear to be in three areas: a sharp reduction in both the expression of threats and physically violent behavior; a better relationship with his immediate family and reconciliation with his oldest child; and a realization that he can now choose whether or not to abort his feelings of agitation before they turn to anger and violence.

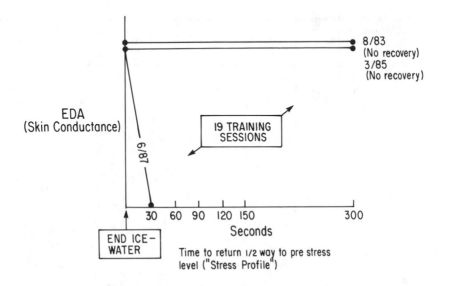

Figure 13.10. *Mr. C's recovery from stress profile is more rapid as training progresses.*

Name __Mr. C (pretreatment)__ Education __College Graduate__ Marital Status __M 2nd wife__ Referred by __Dr. S.__

Date __8/26/81__ Age __34__ Occupation __Disabled (30% Service -connected)__ Presenting Problems __Violent behavior, Pain__

5'9"; 145 lbs

STIMULI	PRESUMED INTERNAL PROCESSES	TARGET PROBLEMS	TREATMENT METHODS	EVALUATION METHODS
Memories of combat in Vietnam, of being a POW, being raped, a victim.	Frustration, Humiliation Self-Esteem Decreases Anger Anxiety	Violent Behavior Many fights with fists, knives, and guns. Has been convicted of manslaughter. Carries a knife at all times. Keeps a gun in his car. Frequently threatens.	Relaxation, Bio-feedback, anger management and pain management training. Alcohol Rehabiliation Program (Client refuses to attend)	Record keeping best and worst experiences each day. Psychophysiological monitoring SCL = .55 - .71. Monitor pain levels, sleep, etc.
Veterans Administration Denied increase in disability payment. Financial Prob Crowds	Self-Concept: "I can't relax"; "I can't get close to people"; "I was terrorized"; "I have no conscience"; "I am a loner"; "I don't lie but I've been lied to all my life".	Substance Abuse Current marijuana, and alcohol, occasional cocaine. Previously Heroin, cocaine and alcohol.	Vietnam Vets Group (sporadic attendance) Elavil "has helped with some of these problems" (Wants Demerol)	#Arrests = 1 (2 mo. ago), #Days in Jail = 1, #Threats = 7+ last week,

Wife ("hassles me") Daughters ("one is always sick the other is always in trouble").	Hoped for Possible Selves: Respected, In Control, Rich	Post-Traumatic Stress Disorder Nightmares, sleep disorder, startle response, flash-backs.	Prior Treatments: transcutaneous nerve stimulation, surgery, medication, psychotherapy.	#Grab, shove = 7+, #Hit = 1 time in last week.
Childhood abused by father (and mother).	Feared Possible Selves: Terrorized, Victim, Poor	Chronic Pain Left leg and both arms (still has some shrapnel).	Hopes, Interests, Hobbies: 100% Service connection. Interested in guns, explosives and motorcycles.	Paranoia Scale = Hi; Anger/violence scale = Hi.
Memory of terminating abuse by threatening father with a gun. Developed a reputation as a terrorist and "ready to kill."	Chronic high arousal and high reactivity.	Disability Issues "I want 100% disability-I'm unemployable".		High IQ (Ammons Quick Test) = 130+.
Wounded - shrapnael is still in left arm and leg				Notes: Is articulate, Neurological Work-up / EEG Normal.

Figure 13.9. *Pretreatment flow diagram for Mr. C.*

Name __Mr. C (post-treatment)__ Education __College Graduate__ Marital Status __M 3rd wife__ Referred by __Dr. S.__

Date __8/27/87__ Age __40__ Occupation __Disabled (100% Service__ Presenting Problems __Violent behavior,__

__5'9"; 140 lbs__   __-connected)__   __Pain__

STIMULI	PRESUMED INTERNAL PROCESSES	TARGET PROBLEMS	TREATMENT METHODS	EVALUATION METHODS
Same as in 1981, except he now has 100% Service-Connected Disability and is married to a different woman – "who doesn't hassle me – at least not in the same ways".	Frustration → Anger Self-Esteem decreases Self-Concept: "I have a better family life now", "I'm being screwed financially"; "I've let go of some old problems and solved some tough problems".	Violent Behavior? no fights for 4 months, occasional threats. Substance Abuse? no alcohol for 2 years, no cocaine for 2+ years, marijuana less than once per week.	Follow-up and continuing work on remaining problems, 1 session every 2 weeks. Antabuse	Assign occasional record keeping (compliance is excellent). Psychophysiological monitoring SCL = .25 - .36;
	Hoped for Possible Selves: Respected, In Control, Rich Feared Possible Selves: Victim, Trapped, Poor	PTSD? symptoms persist but somewhat more bearable and less frequent.		Blood flow in arms and legs is asymmetrical–left side lower than right. Monitor pain levels (still Hi).
Financial Problems				

Lower resting arousal and lower reactivity.	Chronic Pain? persists (methadone helps)	Methadone (and other Medications) Hopes, Interests, Hobbies: "I need more money".	Monitor sleep (only slight improvement). Paranoia Scale = Mod-Hi; Anger/Violence Scale = variable (Mod-Hi). Threats = 1 in last week (no hits). Arrests = None in 12 months.

Figure 13.11. *Post-treatment flow diagram for Mr. C*

PERSONAL SCIENCE--FORMAT FOR DEVELOPING A MULTILEVEL **ABC** DIAGRAM:
Use this format to describe the most recent (or most memorable) occurrence of your problem and fill in
as many of the spaces as you can.

ANTECEDENTS: Ask yourself what was going on in yourself and your environment just before
the problem occurred;

BEHAVIORS: Ask yourself what behavior did you show and what was going on in yourself and
environment during the behavioral episode;

CONSEQUENCES: Ask youself what happened after the behavioral episode ended.

		ANTECEDENTS	BEHAVIORS	CONSEQUENCES
THINGS OTHER PEOPLE	DO	debt, bank agent telephones	Listen	Bank sends forclosure
	SAY	"you know you owe us 2000 and what will happen if you don't pay."	"We'll see about that."	
OTHER ENVIRONMENTAL EVENTS		Wife sick, baby sick and crying, daughter in jail		Police "watching me."
MY OVERT BEHAVIOR		sit and listen	Swear at him; threat - "you hassle me again & you've had it." Hang up	"nothing I can do."
MY COVERT BEHAVIOR — THOUGHTS		"got to get them before they get me."	"Get him." "Gather ammo."	"I told him I could kill him." "They'll know who did it."
MOODS, EMOTIONS & FEELINGS		Angry Depressed Anxious	ANGRY	Joy Trapped, angry, depressed, anxious
LABELS I USE FOR MYSELF		Stressed, shafted, trapped, warrior	Warrior	victim, poor, trapped
THE LEVEL OF MY SELF ESTEEM	HIGH			high
	MEDIUM		medium	
	LOW	low		low
THE LEVEL OF MY EXCITEMENT	HIGH	high	high	high
	MEDIUM			
	LOW			

Figure 13.12. *Mr. C - ABC depiction of an episode.*

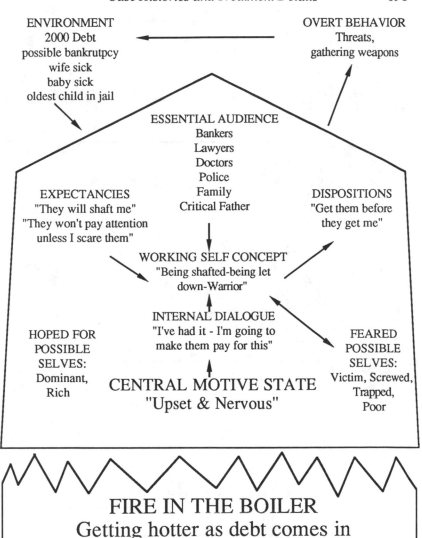

ENVIRONMENT
2000 Debt
possible bankrutpcy
wife sick
baby sick
oldest child in jail

OVERT BEHAVIOR
Threats,
gathering weapons

ESSENTIAL AUDIENCE
Bankers
Lawyers
Doctors
Police
Family
Critical Father

EXPECTANCIES
"They will shaft me"
"They won't pay attention
unless I scare them"

DISPOSITIONS
"Get them before
they get me"

WORKING SELF CONCEPT
"Being shafted-being let
down-Warrior"

INTERNAL DIALOGUE
"I've had it - I'm going to
make them pay for this"

HOPED FOR
POSSIBLE
SELVES:
Dominant,
Rich

FEARED
POSSIBLE
SELVES:
Victim, Screwed,
Trapped,
Poor

CENTRAL MOTIVE STATE
"Upset & Nervous"

FIRE IN THE BOILER
Getting hotter as debt comes in
and other stresses persist

Figure 13.13. *Depiction of Mr. C dealing with same episode as in figures 13.12 and 13.14.*

Name Mr. C   Date 2/7/87   Age 40   Education College Graduate   Occupation Disabled (100% Service-connected)   Marital Status M 3rd wife   Referred by Dr. S.   Presenting Problems Violent behavior, Pain

STIMULI	PRESUMED INTERNAL PROCESSES	TARGET PROBLEMS	TREATMENT METHODS	EVALUATION METHODS
LT ST History Triggers Abused as a child Negatively reinforced as a terrorist Financial problems $2,000 Debt Family Problems	Self-Concept (working): "Terrorist; I've been shafted; I'm fed up; I'm wired". Hoped for Possible Selves: Hero, Feared, Respected, Rich Feared Possible Selves: Victim, Raped, Scorned, Poor Expectancies "They will shaft me"; "They won't pay attention unless I scare or hurt them."	Violent Behavior Threats (I've killed before and I'll kill again–in a second"). Impulse Control Problems Substance Abuse Alcohol (not for 24 months) Marijuana (3x last week Cocaine (?), etc.	Anger management program (biofeedback, relaxation, cognitive behavior therapy, stress management) On Antabuse (won't go to AA) (won't go to NA)	Count # threats. Self report on: anger, violence, anxiety, depression, pain, etc.

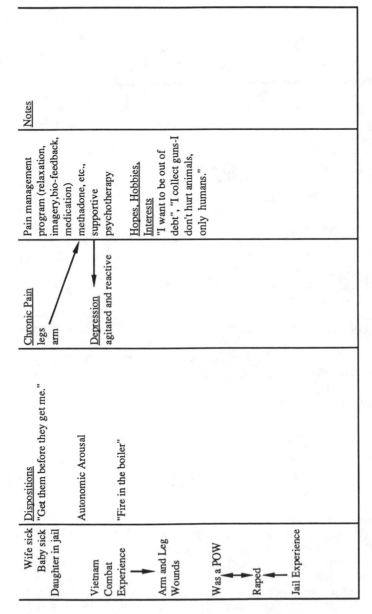

Figure 13.14. *Flow diagram of Mr. C dealing with same episode as in Figures 13.12 and 13.13.*

Mr. D

Mr. D, a 27-year-old man with a high-school education and a verbal IQ of over 125 (Wechsler Adult Intelligence Scale), was known to the police in his small southern Vermont town as someone who occasionally made threats with weapons. He had also spent a few months in psychiatric hospitals (for problems related to anxiety and impulse control). His status at the time of assessment is shown in Figure13.15. Mr. D is five feet, 10 inches tall, and he weighed 150 pounds at the start of treatment.

Part of Mr. D's case history was presented in Chapter 6 (in connection with his treatment for abuse of his preverbal step-daughter). Further details of his background follow. Mr. D is the oldest of five children. Both of his parents are still alive, and his father is an alcoholic. Prior to entering the service, Mr. D's social behavior was within normal limits and he did well in school. While Mr. D was serving in Vietnam with the Army, he experienced a head injury while working on a tank. This appears to have been a turning point in his life. Since that time, much of his behavior can be characterized as disorganized and impulsive. He has lapses of memory and judgment and he is frequently unkempt. Mr. D's neurological exam with EEG was indicative of diffuse neurological impairment. Neuropsychological evaluations using the Halstead Reitan Battery also indicate diffuse neurological impairment. When Mr. D was about to be discharged from the service, he met and married a 16-year-old girl who was pregnant with another man's child.

At the time of referral to us for neuropsychological assessment and treatment for anxiety-related problems, Mr. D was not a member of an organized religion. He later joined a fundamentalist church and often gives credit to the church for "cleaning up my act." At the time of referral, Mr. D held occasional odd jobs and earned about $2,000 a year, which was supplemented by a service-connected disability payment of several hundred dollars a month. This income was insufficient to meet the family's expenses, and they were having trouble with both the water supply and the heating system in their small house. They were not able to afford an automobile, and Mr. D had no driver's license. Mr. D spent much of his time hunting and fishing. Shortly after the end of the treatment described in Chapter 6, Mr. D came to us saying that he was considering killing one of his neighbors and had publicly threatened to shoot this man with a rifle. The apparent stimulus for this threat was the neighbor's statement that he would "keep your wife warm while you are in the hospital." Mr. D inferred from this that his neighbor was going to try to seduce Mr. D's wife while Mr. D was in the hospital for elective surgery (for a hernia). Shortly after Mr. D's confession of this threat to us, we learned that he had frequently threatened his wife and many other people (see Figure 13.16). While he had rarely carried out his threats, many in his neighborhood were afraid of him. His immediate family suffered the brunt of his anger and threats. When Mr. D was angry with someone outside the family, he would talk of nothing else but the details of his plans for revenge. Following an altercation, Mr. D would stay angry for at least two days, and he would get little sleep during this period. Because of the fact that most people took Mr. D very seriously, they would stay away from him, or they would somehow let him know that they were intimidated by his threats. One individual told Mr. D something like "I know you're crazier than I am, and you might just do it."

Much of the treatment of Mr. D has been described in parts of other chapters and is summarized below. Mr. D was unable to follow, or uninterested in following, the sort of complex mini model shown in Figures 13.16, 13.17 and 13.18. The first two of these depict his general stance in response to many social situations. The last depicts a specific episode when his wife had a miscarriage. He only occasionally participated in development of such models and responded best to the simplest – such as shown in Figure 13.16. The treatment procedure that appeared to have the greatest impact on Mr. D was the training in autonomic control during stress interviews and the extension of this training into real-life settings by way of a simple recipe (described in detail in Chapter 3). Mr. D learned to detect high levels, and shifts in the level, of his emotional fire in the boiler. He was able to use this learning to almost always respond effectively to the following command: "When you notice the fire in the boiler say, 'I'm upset,' and then quickly start using your relaxation response to lower the fire in the boiler." His frequent rehearsal of this simple formula led to changes in his behavior outside the treatment setting and laid the foundation for the development of a new working self-concept, with attendant changes in expectancies and dispositions, and with occasional adaptive internal dialogue. An important feature of Mr. D's treatment was a review and discussion at the end of each session of the graph of autonomic function during the session. He became very accurate at perceiving shifts in his autonomic arousal and became justifiably proud of his ability. He would often take several copies of the graphs home with him to show other people.

The present status of Mr. D is dramatically changed since the end of the period described in Chapter 6; his current status is shown in Figure 13.19. His wife has left him, and he has a new live-in girlfriend. He is no longer in touch with his stepdaughter or his two sons, and although he misses them, he says "maybe it's for the best that they get a new start." Mr. D is currently employed part-time as a laborer, but is noting persistent memory problems. His family is concerned with a continuing weight loss (he now weighs 135 pounds) and apparent sadness (which he denies to us). They also note that he has not expressed any anger for the past nine months and has made no threats since April 30, 1986 (a year-and-a-half prior to the moment at which I am writing this account).

For Mr. D we can identify no specific instance of the operation of negative reinforcement prior to the onset of his violent behavior. Therefore we must assume that the head injury in Vietnam has much to do with his present status. Of the four clients presented in this chapter, Mr. D is least likely to profit from considering mini models and theories regarding his own personality. However, his relatively high level of intellectual function in some areas, and his development of skill at controlling autonomic responses to previously anger-provoking situations, permitted us to use many of the same treatment procedures that we employed with the other three men.

	Antecedents	Behaviors	Consequences (short term)
Mr. D.	Someone behaves so as to cause client to have the (expected) perception that he is being ignored or otherwise belittled	Yell, Threaten and/or Hit	Opponent Attends, Responds, Retreats or Otherwise Submits → Society and/ or Opponent actively avoids or otherwise isolates client

Figure 13.16. *Prototypical ABC sequence when Mr. D yells, threatens and/or hits.*

Name Mr. D (pre-treatment)   Education High School   Marital Status Married   Referred by Ward

Date 1975   Age 27   Occupation Laborer (60% Service   -connected)   Presenting Problems Violent behavior, anxiety

5'10"; 150lbs

STIMULI	PRESUMED INTERNAL PROCESSES	TARGET PROBLEMS	TREATMENT METHODS	EVALUATION METHODS
Head Injury (1968)	Organic Damage	Memory Impairment	Tailored Vocational Rehab	Annual - Halstead, WAIS, Weschler Memory
	? ?	Seizures ?	Medication	Monthly - blood levels of medication
Family "Problems" (money, job, finances, etc.)	ANXIETY Self esteem GUILT drops ANGER	"Rage" Attacks i.e., Violent Behavior and Threats	Cognitive behavioral therapy and biofeedback (for arousal detection and control)	Bi - Weekly evaluation of data sheets
Child Crying	SELF-CONCEPT "I'm pretty smart" "I'm a good shot"	Speech Problems		
Child "Misbehavior" 1) rock throwing 2) bed wetting 3) fighting (etc)	"? no identity" - "nothing" "must be in control" High resting arousal and high reactivity	CHILD ABUSE 1) hitting 2) scolding and controlling 3) threats 4) ignore–unless child "misbehaves."	Family counsel and behavior therapy	Psychophysiological monitoring (SCL = .55 - .9). Threats (=7+ last week), Hits (= 4x last week),

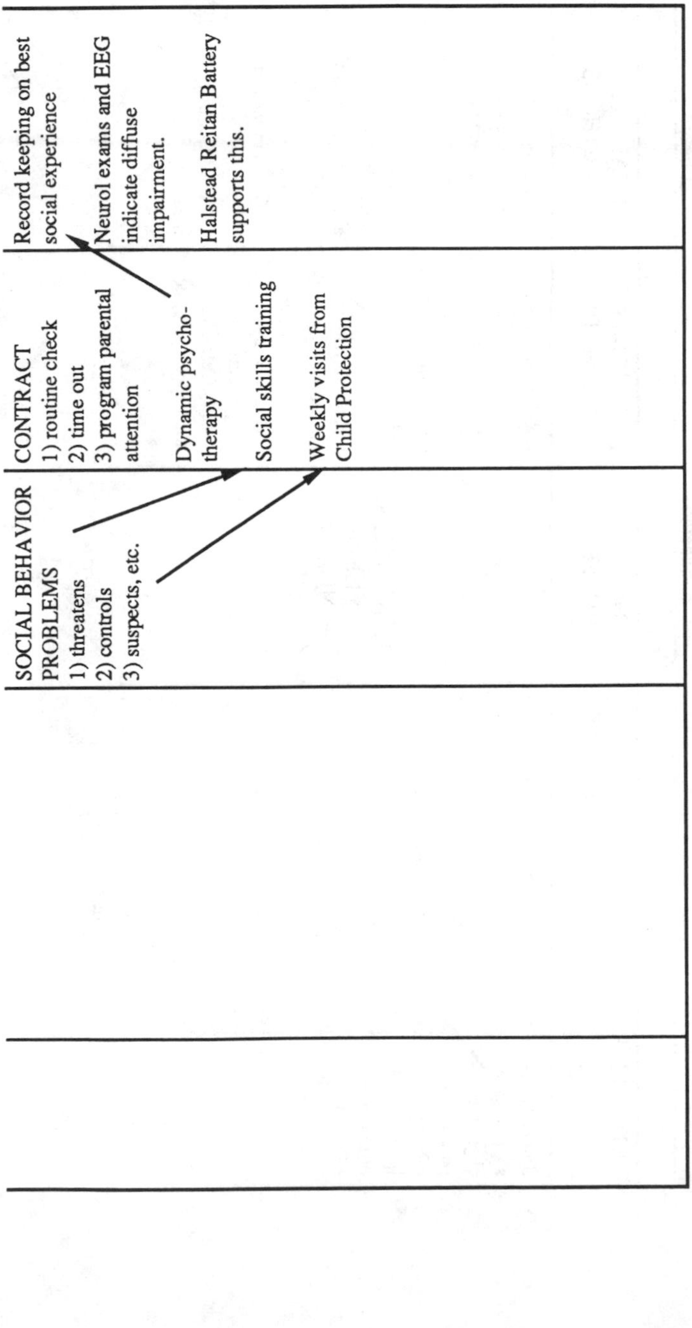

Figure 13.15. *Pre-treatment flow diagram for Mr. D.*

Name Mr. D   Education High School   Marital Status Married   Referred by Ward

Date 1975   Age 27   Occupation Laborer (60% Service   Presenting Problems Violent behavior, anxiety

5'10"; 150lbs   -connected)

STIMULI	PRESUMED INTERNAL PROCESSES	TARGET PROBLEMS	TREATMENT METHODS	EVALUATION METHODS
Someone acts so as to give client the perception of being ignored or otherwise belittled	Expects people to be rude, (i.e., low self-esteem and low trust). Perceptual Processing → Lowered Self-Esteem → Self-Concept Memories and Fears of 1. being a victim; 2. being humiliated; 3. loss of control; Fears "Anger"	THREATEN, YELL AND/OR HIT	1. Relaxation Training 2. Biofeedback 3. Cognitive behavior therapy 4. Role playing and biofeedback 5. Homework assignments (e.g., Q Calm, say "I'm upset"; practice	Record keeping -most severe anger episode each day -best experience of the day Stress Profiles a) general/ standardized b) individualized Self-esteem measures Locus of Control measures

apologizing; help
someone without
"pay"; tell them it's
because it makes you
feel good.)

Memories of relief (via
"identification with the aggressor")
i.e., via behavioral outburst

<u>DISPOSED</u> TO DO IT AGAIN i.e.,
"ALWAYS READY"

HIGH FIRE IN THE BOILER

Figure 13.17. *Mr. D's general stance in social situations and our plans for treatment and assessment (including the sequence shown in Figures 13.16 and 13.18).*

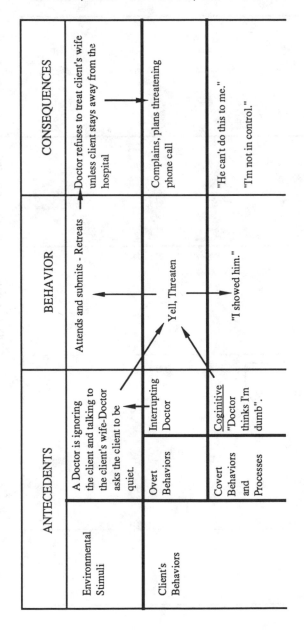

ANTECEDENTS			BEHAVIOR	CONSEQUENCES
Environmental Stimuli		A Doctor is ignoring the client and talking to the client's wife-Doctor asks the client to be quiet.	Attends and submits - Retreats	Doctor refuses to treat client's wife unless client stays away from the hospital
Client's Behaviors	Overt Behaviors	Interrupting Doctor	Yell, Threaten	Complains, plans threatening phone call
	Covert Behaviors and Processes	Coginitive "Doctor thinks I'm dumb".	"I showed him."	"He can't do this to me." "I'm not in control."

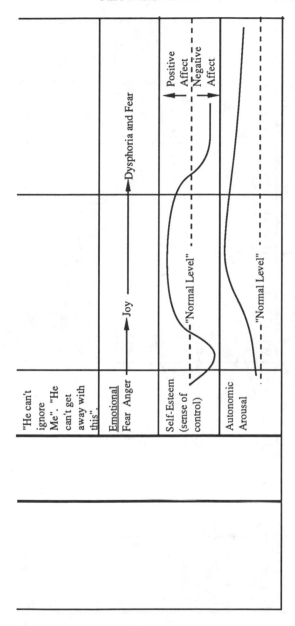

Figure 13.18. *Multilevel ABC diagram of Mr. D's "problem in the hospital" when his wife had a miscarriage (a specific example of the generalizations shown in Figures 13.16 and 13.17).*

Name __Mr. D (post-treatment)__ Education __High School__ Marital Status __woman__ Referred by __Ward__

Date __1987__ Age __39__ Occupation __Laborer (Disabled) (60%__ Presenting Problems __Violent behavior,__

5' 10"; 135 lbs   Service – Connected)   Divorced: living with a   anxiety

STIMULI	PRESUMED INTERNAL PROCESSES	TARGET PROBLEMS	TREATMENT METHODS	EVALUATION METHODS
Head Injury (1968)	Organic Damage	Memory Impairment	Ongoing tailored vocational rehab	Job performance
Family "Problems" (money, job, finances, etc.)	? ?	Seizures (under control)	Medication	Occasional blood levels of medication
	ANXIETY GUILT ANGER	?Thoughts of doing violence	Follow-up sessions biofeedback (for arousal detection and control)	Occasional Weschler Memory Test
		Speech Problems		
	SELF-CONCEPT "I'm getting by" "I believe in Jesus" "I've got a good woman" "I miss the kids"	Depression? Weight loss? Social Behavior Problems 1) withdraws	Occasional follow-up family counsel and behavior therapy and cognitive behavior therapy	

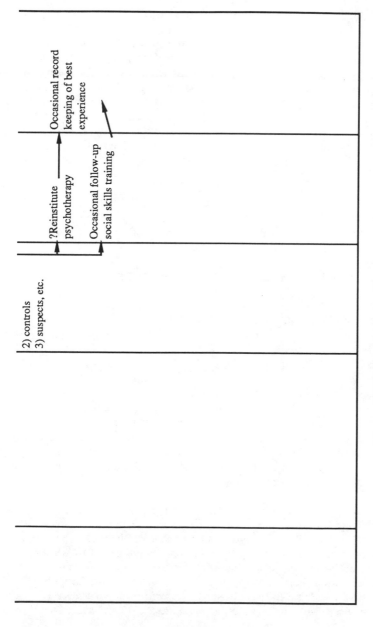

Figure 13.19. *Post-treatment flow diagram for Mr. D.*

Treatment Adaptations

We have worked with a number of clients who have been unable to profit from full application of the general method for treatment. For these clients, we adapt our overall method, or we may employ only one technique out of the array. For example, the one-sentence rationale used with Mr. D has been a helpful core intervention with some very difficult organically impaired individuals. I will present excerpts of the treatment records of two violent clients for whom we have substantially adapted the general method. I will then review the case of Ms. E, for whom I applied directly the personality theory I have outlined earlier in this book.

Mr. G

The following is a slightly abridged copy of a final report used with one such client:

Psychology Section (116B) X456 Patient Report: Mr. G

Date: 1/86 Therapist: John A. Corson, Ph.D.

ASSESSMENT

Extensive assessment (described elsewhere) indicates diffuse organic impairment – somewhat more impairment in frontal lobes than elsewhere – considerable memory impairment – and near – or above – normal performance in some areas (e.g., verbal IQ as indexed by Ammons Quick Test of Intelligence). His performance on some standard neuropsychological tests indicates *impairment unless* he is in a quiet and familiar environment – and then he can perform within the normal range. For example, on the Wisconsin Card Sort Test – which is a standard tool for assessing frontal lobe impairment, addition of a white noise (radio static – at a mildly noxious level) raises his error rate from 23% (normal) to 50% (profoundly impaired). On the Digit Span Test of the Wechsler Memory Scale he was not influenced by white noise, but when two relative strangers came into the room during testing his score dropped (from 9 to 6). On another test – the Category Test from the Halstead Reitan Battery – he performed in the severely impaired range unless he was asked to reconsider the rules, and heard the instructions reiterated when he expressed confusion or began to respond randomly (his Categories performance and its implications are discussed in detail elsewhere). The basic point here is that he is impaired – and his greatest impairment is shown in noisy or confusing situations. If he can remain calm, work in a quiet, familiar, and structured environment, with occasional prompts regarding rules and objectives, he should do quite well.

Conclusions from Psychometric and Behavioral Observations since 9/19/83:

Mr. G shows psychometric and behavioral signs of impairment that are made much worse whenever some form of social stimulation (e.g., strange people, demands, humiliation) is combined with a high noise level in the environment and/or confusion regarding what is expected of Mr. G ("cognitive noise"). These conditions rapidly lead to a high arousal state which Mr. G is often unable to manage in an adaptive manner.

(Note on arousal state: During white noise and psychological testing on 6/3/86 Mr. G's skin conductance level went from 7 micro mho – normal level – to 50 micro mho – a level we rarely have seen in anyone. At the end of the session, his hands were soaking wet.)

BEHAVIORAL MANAGEMENT PROPOSAL:

As indicated above, Mr. G should be placed in a quiet, structured, and supportive environment – where staff personnel are trained to provide prompts regarding rules and objectives. (Specific vocational training suggestions are provided elsewhere – e.g., see report of 11/85.) Specific behavioral management procedures are as follows:

I. The Quick Calming Response

Mr. G has been asked to *practice* the quick calming response: *"Practice calming down for two breaths – breathe a little deeper than usual; on the outbreath think the word "calm" and smile to yourself; breathe in again – a little more deeply than usual – on the outbreath say the word "calm" to yourself and smile to yourself."*

He has been asked to practice this whenever he hears his watch "beep" (every 1/2 hour), and whenever he hears a telephone ring, and whenever he looks at a watch or a clock, and whenever he goes to the bathroom. This will result in *more than a dozen practice episodes per day*, and will keep the calming response ready for use if he gets upset. *He should be reminded of this daily.*

II. The Anger/Frustration/Confusion Management Strategy

In response to feelings of anger or frustration or confusion, Mr. G has been trained to use the general strategy of (1) *saying* (quietly) "I'm upset" and then (2) *doing* the quick calming response. Following the announcement of his being upset and the quick calming response (taking about 20 seconds) he is to (3) quietly problem solve with the most appropriate person(s). *He should be reminded of this daily.*

III. The Role-Playing Strategy

Whenever Mr. G shows signs of being upset, a role- playing session should be conducted – along with a reminder that he must be responsible for his self-control. In the role-playing session (2-5 minutes), a staff person should reenact the problematic situation with Mr. G and remind him of the quick calming/anger management strategies, and then show him one or two more calm and more adaptive ways of coping with the same situation. (While Mr. G was at the VA Hospital in 1984, we found that it was necessary to repeat such role playing and advice [involving *quick calming* and *anger management strategy*] at least three times after each episode of upset; when he was here in 1985, he did not become upset to the extent of being disruptive.)

Mr.K

Mr. K was not physically violent, but was verbally belligerent. For him, we used a variation of the above procedure. This is spelled out in the following abstract from reports:

Psychology Section (116B) Patient Report: Mr. K

Date: 8/86   Therapist: John A. Corson, Ph.D.

ASSESSMENT

Extensive assessment (described elsewhere) *indicates organic impairment* that apparently resulted from injuries received in 1972.

Organic Impairment – Performance Changes With Time of Day:

Mr. K retains considerable ability in some areas (e.g., vocabulary) but has considerable difficulty in other areas (e.g., motor coordination, concentration, and memory). Over the last few months, we have determined that his problems get worse in the late afternoon and evening. We used a test of eye-hand coordination which showed that Mr. K performs at approximately 80% of the normal level before 2 P.M. and performs at between 20 and 40% of the normal level after 5 P.M.

TREATMENT PLAN

Behavior Which Interferes With Performance in the Workplace--An Extinction Plan:

I have had extensive discussions with Mr. K's employer and supervisor. They have informed me that he has managed to be a good employee "as long as he keeps his mouth under control." We developed a plan with Mr. D of vocational rehabilitation and presented it to Mr. K's employer. The plan is spelled out in the following paragraph:

> Mr. K's employer and co-workers have noted that Mr. K has a tendency to argue and talk too much and/or talk about the wrong things. We have developed an "extinction" procedure which involves explaining to Mr. K the difficulty regarding arguing too much/talking too much/talking about the wrong things/"beating a dead horse", etc., and we made an agreement with Mr. K. This agreement – presented by Mr. K's supervisor (with the knowledge and consent of Mr. K) – was phrased as follows: *"In the past we have had trouble with your arguing or talking too much, or harping on things. So that we can work together effectively we need to make a new arrangement. I propose whenever I feel that you are talking too much, arguing too much, harping, or otherwise being unproductive in conversation I will raise my hand and you*

must stop. The other side of this coin is that you can do the same to me. If you feel that I am talking too much, or harping on something that you already understand you can raise your hand and I will stop. If either of us fails to stop at the sign of the raised hand the other one should simply walk away. If we can understand this as a constructive agreement, entered into by two adults we should be able to make this work. This is a way of me teaching you about what irritates other people. You have had trouble with this in the past, and I am going to do my best to help you improve so that I, and other people, will be able to get along with you more easily.

Results of the Extinction Procedure – A New Two-Part Plan:

The above procedure worked for a while, but eventually the employer complained that "the stop signal only stops him temporarily – and he always seems to have an excuse to start up again right away." On the basis of this information we developed a new two-part procedure which combined the stop signal with a quick relaxation exercise (which Mr. K had learned earlier). The instructions to Mr. K were as follows:

To Mr. K from Dr. Corson:

When you and I met this morning we discussed some problems and put together a new program. This letter summarizes our discussion and plan – please use it as a reminder.

First, you and I agreed that it is important for you to maintain the attitude that you and your employer are working together on a rehabilitation program.

This program is designed to help you cope with your organic and behavioral problems to the extent that you will be able to stay in the workforce. You and I have worked for a long time on a relaxation strategy (the quick calming response) which you must now remember to use whenever you see the "stop signal." You have a well-practiced relaxation response which will help you keep from quickly starting up again. We also expect that the quick calming response will keep you from becoming overly upset about minor hassles at work.

Remember that whenever you receive the "stop signal" (the raised hand) you must use the quick calming response – focus on your breathing – take a deeper than normal breath and breathe out through your nose – smile calmly to yourself. Let a warm comfortable sensation develop in your hands and stomach. Do it again. Each breath takes about ten seconds; the whole exercise takes about 20 seconds. At the end of this quick calming response notice how much better you feel.

Remember that you must practice the quick calming response at times other than when you see the "stop signal". You should be doing it at least 12 times a day. To help yourself to get enough practice you should do the quick calming response each time you look at a watch or a clock, each time you enter a bathroom, and each time you hear a telephone ring.

As you consistently practice the quick calming response (at least 12 times a day) you will notice that the calmness you feel during the response will last longer and longer. You will notice that you are able to calm down more quickly after you see the "stop signal." You will also notice that you will be able to use the quick calming response to quiet yourself down quickly after feeling tension and stress. Remember – practice makes perfect; practice 12 times a day on your own; use the quick calming response whenever you see the stop signal; use the quick calming response whenever you feel tension or stress coming on.

Both Mr. G and Mr. K had experienced head injuries that were documentable by neuropsychological testing and neurological exam, as well as by EEG. They did not seem to profit as much from the biofeedback training as had Mr. D, but they did make some gains, at least in terms of developing a sense of control over themselves in response to this training.

Ms. E

Another seemingly intractable case involved a severely troubled and extremely violent young woman. Ms. E had been able to get through two years at a university even though she had begun to show episodic periods of psychosis in her early teenage years.

These episodes of psychotic behavior included inflicting severe injuries on herself and on others. At the time of my involvement in this case, Ms. E was incarcerated in the secure psychiatric unit of a maximum-security facility. I did not visit with the woman, but discussed her history and status with two senior psychiatrists who knew her case well. I made the following set of suggestions, which I understand have led to (at least a temporary) improvement in her behavior. Ms. E has been able to return to an open ward in a state hospital, and seven months after this program was implemented she was able to spend the weekend with her family. An abridged version of my consultation report follows:

Date: 2/87

To. Dr. W

From: John A. Corson, Ph.D.

Re: Consultation regarding Ms. E, currently housed at Secure Psychiatric Unit

From conversations with Drs. X and Y, I have learned some details of Ms. E's history, medical and psychiatric status, current behavior, and prospects.

I spoke with Dr. X on 2/5/87, and offered the following observations and suggestions:

1. Return of Ms. E to the State Hospital seems advisable even though future violent behavior seems quite likely;
2. An assessment/compilation of activities and specific staff people she has previously shown signs of enjoying(e.g., those she has chosen to spend time with) should be put together;
3. On the basis of this assessment, a long-term management program might be put together along the following lines:

    A. Ms. E should be given reliable clock-contingent attention from someone(preferably someone she seems to enjoy) on each shift (this could be a 10-minute conversation at every hour – a timer should be set so this is not omitted at any time during the day and evening shifts);

B. Whenever possible she should be given opportunity to engage in some enjoyable activity – and she should be given positive attention for doing these activities (in other words, give her opportunities to do good things, and show her some enthusiasm when she is observed doing good things);

C. Whenever she misbehaves, she should be given only the level of perfunctory attention necessary to protect her and others, while clearly informing her of the category of unacceptable behavior that has occurred, and why it is unacceptable, and what a specific appropriate alternative behavior might be. These should not be occasions for extra attention and/or emotionally loaded interactions – her needs for interaction and attention should be satisfied by aspects A and B.

The most important key to this program is aspect 3A. If this is reliably provided, the other aspects should be relatively easy to implement. From my understanding of Ms. E's history and prior treatment, the idea that any additional program features should be aimed at punishing Ms. E, or at teaching her by way of punishment (physical or verbal) not to hurt herself or others, should be abandoned.

This total program should be continued systematically for the duration of her stay at the State Hospital. Any additional rehabilitative or therapeutic features should be seen as add-on features.

Please let me know if you have any questions or observations regarding these suggestions.

From reading the report on Ms. E, you may have recognized some of the principles spelled out in earlier chapters. In particular, I made use of the following ideas:

(1) Individuals are addicted to attention.
(2) Attention must be dissociated from episodes of negative behavior, and, preferably, must also become independent of specific episodes of positive behavior. That is,

attention must become automatic and reliable, and some caution must be taken to make sure that the attention does not come so close in time to a particular episode of negative behavior that it appears to be contingent on that behavior.

(3)   Episodes of misbehavior must be dealt with so as to insure safety, but only with application of the minimum necessary perfunctory attention.

(4)   The attention given for misbehavior must be informationally strong – it must clearly specify the category of unacceptable behavior that has occurred.

(5)   The environment must be structured so as to allow the client maximum opportunity to indulge in enjoyable activities that are appropriate to normal adults of their age.

14 : Theoretical Perspectives and Practical Advice

Now I invite you to reflect on all of the foregoing material and to consider a developmental theory of violent behavior. Then I will offer answers to two perennial questions.

Self–Concept and Violent Behavior

During the initial interview, or in early treatment sessions, almost all 62 of the clients with whom I am most familiar reported some form of traumatic experience early in life. This usually involved chronic physical abuse at the hands of parents, foster parents, or other caretakers. This abuse was usually accompanied by negative labels (such as coward or liar) and led to humiliation, low self-esteem, and assorted negative expectancies regarding both self and others. A very frequent feature in the history, usually between the age of 9 and 15, was an episode in which the client struck back at the tormentor(s) with such vigor that the torment was ended (at least temporarily).

On the basis of my observations of these and other violent clients, I have developed a variation on the developmental sequence[1] presented in Chapter 4; this variation is shown here in Figures 14.1 and 14.2. It seems likely that the first few weeks of most infants' lives have similar impact to that shown in Chapter 4.

[1] Many other theories have been offered to explain developmental influences which might lead to violent adult behavior; a good summary is provided by Hays et al. (1981).

The parental attention becomes a powerful conditioned incentive stimulus, and the process of addicting the child to parental attention begins. However, at the stage depicted by Figure 4.5 in Chapter 4, clear difficulties begin to occur. Specifically, the child is learning that he or she is "not OK." As shown in Figure 4.7 of Chapter 4, this self- labeling eventually becomes independent of behavior. The figures here characterize some important aspects of the development of our typical client. Parental attention is typically negative, with positive attention having more to do with the parents' moods than with the child's behavior. Very early severe beatings typically occur, accompanied by negative labeling of the child. Often in addition to the beatings, prolonged periods of torment are inflicted, which may involve restriction, or even incarceration of the child in dark closets or trunks. The parent apparently responds to the child's crying and other behaviors as if they were personal insults to which the parent must respond.

In reviewing the case histories, I am reminded of Alice Miller's book For Your Own Good (1984), in which the causes of violence are traced to an unequal power struggle between the parent and child. The parent justifies abuse by saying it is "for the good of the child," "an essential part of child-rearing." An important idea in Miller's book is the idea that the tendency to be abusive is passed from one generation to the next generation: "For parents' motives are the same today as they were then; in beating their children they are struggling to regain the power they once lost to their own parents" (page 16).

Eventually, as is shown here in Figure 14.1, the child grows larger and can retaliate effectively in response to an episode of torment. When retaliation is effective in terminating the torment, this mobilizes the mechanism of negative reinforcement (the termination of an aversive stimulus by a behavior increases the future probability of that behavior). Subsequently, the child may tend to become violent in response to a hint of humiliation, a loss of self-esteem, or the like. In fact, this pivotal episode of negative reinforcement seems to galvanize a whole new working self-concept.

As discussed in Chapter 2 a possible self puts a particular working self into action. In this case, the possible self is highly salient, repeatedly experienced, and feared, the feared possible self of the tormented and cowering victim. The relationship between the feared self and the new working self is established by the sudden realization (which may not be conscious in the usual sense of that

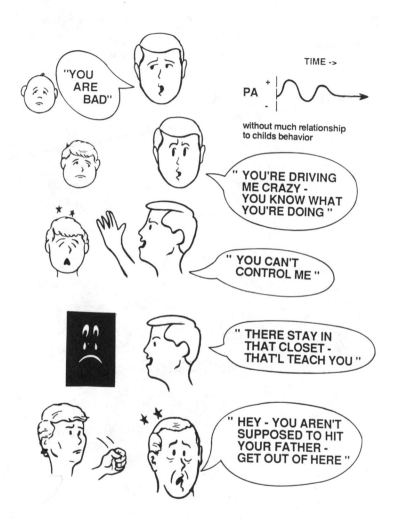

Figure 14.1. *Variation on the developmental sequence - 1.*

" I'M ALWAYS READY"

(Expectancy)

"I'M A WARRIOR"

(Disposition)

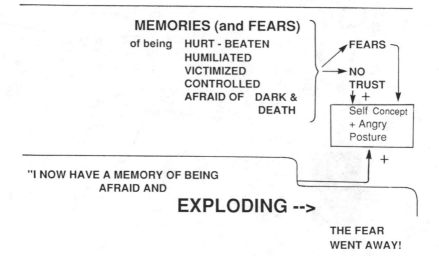

MEMORIES (and FEARS)

of being   HURT - BEATEN
HUMILIATED
VICTIMIZED
CONTROLLED
AFRAID OF   DARK &
DEATH

FEARS
NO
TRUST
+
Self Concept
+ Angry
Posture

+

"I NOW HAVE A MEMORY OF BEING
AFRAID AND

EXPLODING -->

THE FEAR
WENT AWAY!

I WAS IN CONTROL!

I WAS A HERO!   THE CRITICS APPLAUDED!

NOW I'M READY - NO ONE MESSES WITH ME . . . ."

(ie - "I'M BAD - A JUNK YARD DOG")

Figure 14.2. *Variation on the developmental sequence - 2.*

term) that there is a response in their repertoire (violent behavior) that has the guaranteed positive outcome of ending suffering.

Now, as Figure 14.2 shows, here a transformation has occurred – from terrorized to terrorist, with appropriately transformed expectancies and dispositions. The biopsychosocial patterns that are established by this transformation result in a self-perpetuating positive feedback loop. Now, any sign of a feared self, or in some clients even a feeling of upset or dysphoria, will put the working self-concept of the violent warrior into action. This suddenly shifts the dynamics in the system (see the system depicted in Figure 3.1 of Chapter 3) to select which expectancies are present and which dispositions are played out. And this is the basis of the binary-switch mode of behavior. The case histories help illustrate this.

From the above, one might conclude that these clients are all very large and strong, but this is not the case. Even very small people can develop in this manner. The control they exercise over many other people is based on their communication that they will fight to the point of dying – or will kill their opponent at the slightest provocation.

Response to the Violent Person

In these final paragraphs, I will consider two questions that people invariably ask when I make presentations on the subject of violent behavior:

(1) How do you deal with individuals who are threatening to do violence to others?
(2) How do you deal with individuals who are threatening to do violence to you?

When Someone Threatens Others

Much has been written on this topic. What I can add will primarily reinforce what I have found to be valuable in the published literature and folklore. When I am faced with a client threatening to do violence to someone else, my stance is to attempt to validate their feelings of upset, and to attend to the disruptions in self-concept so as to make them feel less alone, and perhaps to feel somewhat more "understood". With many clients part of this task involves determining details of the stressful stimulus or – as some of my combat veteran clients have called it – *the incoming fire*. We can imagine the sequence from the incoming fire to the outgoing fire to be a linear temporal sequence. I work to draw a curtain, or barrier between the temporal point of sensing a feeling of upset and disruption in self-concept, on the one hand, and, on the other, the point of feeling anger, and/or the planning of retaliatory violent behavior. The following depicts this temporal sequence:

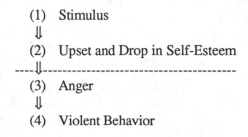

    (1) Stimulus
      ⇓
    (2) Upset and Drop in Self-Esteem
    ----⇓---
    (3) Anger
      ⇓
    (4) Violent Behavior

I have frequently shared such a diagram with clients who are threatening to do violence.

I once heard an address by a psychiatrist who was experienced in dealing with violent individuals, one of his admonitions was to "get on the same side of the fence as the patient with regard to the stimulus issues, but avoid validating the response plans." (This is not a direct quote and is actually a rather bad paraphrase of his more poetic statement – I wish I could remember what he really said.)

Of course if the client continues with the plan to do violence I discuss and, if necessary, initiate appropriate and legally mandated protective steps.

When Someone Threatens You

I have been directly threatened a few dozen times and thus far I have not been attacked. My strategy is to face directly toward the threatening individual without changing posture dramatically. I particularly refrain from standing up while the client is seated. I make it clear to the client that I am going to patiently listen to what he or she has to say.

I also use some self-control procedures with regard to facial expression and eye contact. I believe that these make the client perceive me as being neither threatened or threatening, but simply as an interested person.

Generally, I try to maintain an attitude which is in accord with the previously described theoretical position. Specifically the individual who is moved to threaten another is expressing a working self-concept under highly stressful circumstances. That working self-concept maybe clearly understood if I am careful to ask the right questions and make the right responses. In fact, an episode of being threatened sometimes provides an outstanding opportunity to move ahead in the therapeutic endeavor. In this respect, I maintain a posture of optimism and openness.

15 : Conclusion

We have covered much ground in this consideration of stress, self-concept, and violence. You have been introduced to people, ideas, methods, and data, as well as to anecdotes and hunches. My objective here is to pull it all together, and to identify some remaining problems and possibilities.

Assessment and Treatment

Early in this book, I described a general strategy for developing a new personality theory for each client (Chapter 2). I said that the client and I must work to constantly update the theory so that we are aware of the particular working self-concept that is operating when the client is interacting with a particular stressor. I also said that I would attempt to redefine stressors for each new situation, and that the stress – or impact on the individual – would also need to be reconsidered in each new stressful situation. In other words, the three aspects of the biopsychosocial model (bio, psycho and social) must be considered carefully in each new situation; a change in one domain (say, a change in the bio domain, which is part and parcel of the stress response, or fire in the boiler) would be expected to influence variables in the other two domains (the psycho and the social domains).

Throughout the book, I have attempted to elaborate on methods of updating self-concept and of keeping track of variables in each of the three domains. The following is a review of the strategies I have described for keeping track of the assorted variables. As I illustrated in Chapters 12 and 13, I put these strategies together in a format that will enable me and the particular client to understand what is going on.

We assess the present working self-concept in several ways – most especially by the daily tracking of self-satisfaction and the situations that coincide with the highest and lowest levels of self-satisfaction (see Chapters 7 and 12). A second-order assessment strategy is the frequent review, in the context of the general flow diagram (Chapter 9) of the presumed internal processes and the assorted self-statements that apparently constitute the present working self-concept. I frequently review these self-statements with the client, and we use various strategies to help determine what the current list membership and rank order or weighting should be. (See, for example, Figure 13.18 in Chapter 13.)

When there is a particular identifiable stressor, I may draw a new flow diagram, with new self-referent terms, ordered and weighted to depict the working self-concept interacting with this particular stressor (as in Figure 13.14 of Chapter 13). As mentioned earlier, the stress response (fire in the boiler and central motive state), and the expectancies and dispositions attendant to the working self-concept, can often be elaborated in a telling manner when we are dealing with a particularly compelling stressful situation (as in Figure 13.14 of Chapter 13).

Sometimes I do this work in the context of a conversation, and I draw a flow diagram during the conversation in collaboration with the client (as in Figure 13.15 of Chapter 13). At other times, the multilevel ABC format, depicted in Table 1.1 of Chapter 1, is used to examine and display these various entities and their relationships (see also Figure 13.16 and 13.19 in Chapter 13). As I have so often mentioned, the client and I must collaborate closely if we are going to do our job well. Many times, the particular display or discussion of situation, psychological, biological, and self-concept variables is not interesting or helpful to a client. I will then create a special, or simplified, chart (as in Figure 13.16 of Chapter 13). In some sessions with almost all clients, the lights seem to come on – and the client assumes the stance of the personal theorist. At these times, the client clearly sees a particular working self-concept as the superordinate variable in controlling the fire in the boiler, expectancies, and dispositions. For most clients – at least a few times – such a realization leads to a quantum leap toward considering, and often toward trying out new ways of behaving. Sometimes this leads to new ways of being and new life-styles. When these leaps occur, all of the technical nuts and bolts that I have been describing seem to have been worthwhile.

Biofeedback

I have not proved that our clients are better off for the particular set of strategies I've used – and I've not really proved that the addition of biofeedback had a helpful impact (see Chapter 12). I have no control groups and am forced to cite a set of less-than-optimal supports for my argument that the biofeedback has in fact been helpful:

(1) No client improved while on the waiting list – for periods ranging from one week to three months.
(2) Most clients had previously received many other therapies without achieving a reduction in their violent behavior.
(3) Some clients (e.g., Mr. A) were difficult to communicate with prior to the introduction of biofeedback.
(4) Some clients showed clear correlations of reduction in autonomic levels and reactivities, and durations of episodes of high arousal, with reductions in the level and frequency of their angry feelings and violent behavior.
(5) Among the clients for whom we have data on the effects of biofeedback, we have some evidence (described in Chapter 12) that those who showed the most progress in reducing their autonomic levels and reactivities, and durations of episodes of high arousal also showed the greatest reductions in their violent behavior.
(6) Most of our successful clients have offered testimony about how the biofeedback helped them.

Nevertheless, the relationship is not proven, in the sense that it would be if control groups had been used.[1]

I now leave to you the task of deciding overall whether the outcomes I have described could be achieved more economically, more humanely, or in some better way, by using some other "nuts and bolts."

[1] I have found that, in this work, control groups (other than waiting list controls – and documented periods on other treatment) would be very difficult to match and organize to the extent that they would meet the criteria set by most critics.

Violent Behavior

A more general remaining problem is the disturbing fact--that many of these clients are still terrified and terrifying. Even in my most optimistic moments, I realize that at least some of these individuals will still suffer themselves and will also cause much suffering for others. Their problems are not completely solved.

On the day I write this last chapter, I have had follow-up contact with a sister of one of my clients. She informed me that he has not been violent at any time during the last year. However, he seems miserable and is losing weight. Could it be that the energizing effects of his rage and violent behavior have not been replaced by effective substitutes?

A few weeks ago I had a visit with another client with whom I have not dared to completely sever ties – even though I began to work with him in 1979, and even though he has not had even a minor episode of violent behavior over the last five years. The longest time I have gone without seeing this client is three months – and our follow-up schedule is now rigidly set up, with appointments once every three months. I ask myself why I continue to work with this man, who has taken on a new life-style, and has hurt no one for years. The answer is that I believe he is ready to explode at any moment, and that the follow-up sessions are necessary to keep him practicing his new way of being. He tells me things that are not very comforting:

> I am just as paranoid as I used to be. ...I used to get
> a lot of pleasure out of kicking ass. ...I just realize
> it's not worth it, and I keep my mouth shut whenever
> somebody tries to bother me. ...I've learned to mind
> my own business. ...It's a lot of work for me to stay
> like this. ...It's like my old self is just under the
> surface looking for an excuse to break out – even
> though life is much better now – I'm still just as
> paranoid as I used to be – but I'm less agitated.

Another client told me recently that he had an offer to "hit a guy" (this apparently means that he had an offer of money to kill another person); he told me that the payoff would be $3,000 but that he did not intend to go through with it. He also told me, however, that if he were "driven to the wall" by his financial problems, he might think it over again.

Still another client recently described to me his urges to hurt a physician who had apparently not done a good job of treating his wife. He also described an explosion in public over an Oriental teenager who was employed in a supermarket packing groceries. My client refused to pay for the groceries that were touched by the teenager, and he marched out announcing that he would never shop in the store again. When I think about this particular man (and about many of my other clients), I realize that he has a value system and expectancies and dispositions that are absolutely foreign to me. In my optimistic moments I think we can whittle away at these if we continue working together. In my more pessimistic moments, I think that I, or the client, will be dead before much change is made in many of these domains.

The remaining problems with these clients illustrate the need for continuing development of new assessment and treatment procedures, and also the need for very long-term therapy and follow-up of the violent client.

Personality and Society

More general problems remain in the society that gave rise to such terrified and terrifying people. Much has been written on these broader issues, and I will not add much more. The problems in our society range from child-rearing practices to the examples set by many of our leaders and models. Many of us revere violence, as shown by the popularity of boxing and football and of movies such as Rambo. Throughout recorded history there have been wars, and the tradition of the warrior persists. We have many problems that stem from this tradition: all of the clients described in this book were explicitly trained to be warriors.

I do not have any robust and proven solutions to offer. However, many possibilities come to mind. One of my favorite possibilities is a central theme of this book. Let us try to empower the individual by helping him or her to develop a sense of agency and the attitude of the personal scientist/theorist. Such a sense and such an attitude can help in the development and implementation of strategies for dealing with stressors and stress that are more adaptive and humane than those now typical of most of us. A greater sense of agency and responsibility for one's own life – as well as an appreciation that it is pleasant to have other people be kind to us – should be helpful in ameliorating some of society's persisting problems. When we design and select our therapeutic formats well, we are usually able to set up circumstances that prove to the client that the most sensible way to get other people to be kind is to be kind to them. The format shown in Figure 1.1 of Chapter 1 is often a powerful aid in this endeavor. This is particularly clear when the client is initially unaware of the threatening quality of his or her behavior (facial expression, posture, tone of voice.)

Some of the clinical procedures that have been described in this book might also be used in mainstream educational settings to assist children in developing alternative responses to situations that are likely to be highly stressful and that frequently provoke anger and violence. The kind of role-playing procedures, with use of video-tape, described by Benson, Rice and Miranti (1986) for use with retarded individuals in sheltered workshops, might be adapted for large-scale applications in the school systems. Similarly, some of the strategies for examining the antecedents, behaviors, and conse-quences for a particular individual in a stressful situation (such as that depicted in Table 1.1 of Chapter 1) and some of the strategies used to help clients appreciate the role of the "fire in the boiler" and their own impact on others (as depicted in Figure 3.1 of Chapter 3) might also be fruitfully adapted for use in educational settings. Perhaps such additions to the educational curriculum would help us to counteract some of the negative effects of the warrior tradition. We might even move closer to Freud's ideal (see Chapter 11) of enlarging the population of those seen as potential friends and thus reducing the population of those seen as potential enemies.

References

Adler, A. (1979). *Superiority and social interest* (H.L. Ansbacher and R.R Ansbacher, Eds. and trans.) (3rd rev. ed.). New York: W.W. Norton.

Allport, G.W. (1937). *Personality: A psychological interpretation.* New York: Holt, Rinehart & Winston.

Almy, T.P., & Corson, J.A. (in press 1988). Psychophysiologic observations. In D.A. Drossman (Ed.), *The Patient with Gastrointestinal Complaints.* New York: Grune & Stratton.

Almy, T.P. (1978). The stress intereview: Unfinished business. *Journal of Human Stress,* 4, 3-8.

Ansbacher, H.L., & Ansbacher, R.R. (Eds.). (1956). *The individual psychology of Alfred Adler.* New York: Basic Books.

Atthowe, J.M., Jr. (1973). Token economies come of age: *Behavior Therapy,* 4, 646-654.

Bandura, A. (1969). *Principles of behavior modification.* New York: Holt, Rinehart and Winston.

Bandura, A. (1977). Self-efficacy: Towards a unifying theory of behavioral change. *Psychological Review,* 84, 191-215.

Bandura, A. (1977). *Social learning theory.* Englewood Cliffs, New Jersey: Prentice-Hall.

Bandura, A. (1978). The self system in reciprocal determinism. *American Psychologist,* 33, 344-358.

Bandura, A. (1982). The self and mechanisms of agency. In J. Suls (Ed.), *Psychological perspectives on the self* (Vol. 1, pp. 3-39). Hillsdale, NJ: Lawrence Erlbaum.

Bandura, A. (1982). Self-efficacy mechanism in human agency. *American Psychologist,* 37, 122-147.

Bannister, R. (1982). *Autonomic failure.* New York: Oxford.

Bauer, W.D., & Twentyman, C.T. (1985). Abusing, neglectful and comparison mothers' responses to child-related and non–child-related stressors. *Journal of Consulting and Clinical Psychology,* 53 (3), 335-343.

230   STRESS, SELF-CONCEPT, and VIOLENCE

Benson, H., Beary, J.F., & Carol, M.P. (1974).   The relaxation response. *Psychiatry*, 37, 37-46.
Benson, B.A., Johnson Rice, C., & Miranti, S. V. (1986).   Effects of anger management training with mentally retarded adults in group treatment. *Journal of Consulting and Clinical Psychology*, 54 (5), 728-729.
Berman, P.A., & Johnson, H.J. (1985).   A psychophysiological assessment battery. *Biofeedback and Self Regulation*, 10, 203-221.
Bindra, D. (1959). *Motivation: A systematic reinterpretation*. New York: Ronald Press.
Bindra, D. (1974).   A motivational view of learning, performance, and behavior modification. *Psychological Review*, 81, 199-213.
Block, J. (1971). *Lives through time*. Berkeley, CA: Bancroft Books.
Blumer, D., & Migeon, C. (1975).   Hormone and hormonal agents in the treatment of aggression. *The Journal of Nervous and Mental Disease*, 160 (2), 127-137.
Brett, E.A., & Ostroff, R. (1985).   Imagery and posttraumatic stress disorder: An overview. *The American Journal of Psychiatry*, 141 (4), 417-424.
Brooks, C. McC. (1979).   Present interests in and concepts of autonomic nervous system function. *Journal of the Autonomic Nervous System*, 1 (1) 1-12.
Brooks, C.McC., & Lange, G. (1982).   Patterns of reflex action, their autonomic components, and their behavioral significance. *The Pavlovian Journal of Biological Science*, 17, 55-61.
Buros, O.K. (1974). *Tests in Print II*. Highland Park, NJ: Gryphon.
Cattell, R.B. (1965). *The scientific analysis of personality*. Baltimore: Penguin.
Christopherson, E.R. (1980). The pediatrician and parental discipline. *Pediatrics*, 66, 641-642.
Christopherson, E.R., Kuehn, B.S., Grinstead J.D., et al. (1976). A family training program for abuse and neglect families. *Journal of Pediatric Psychology*, 1, 90-94.
Clark, D.M. (1986). A cognitive approach to panic. *Behavior Research & Therapy*, 24 (4), 461-470.
Cleghorn, R.A. & Pattee, C.J. (1954). Psychologic changes in 3 cases of Addison's Disease during treatment with cortisone. *Journal of Clinical Endocrinology & Metabolism*, 14, 344-352.
Coleman, J.S. (1966). *Equality of educational opportunity*. U.S. Government Printing Office, Washington, D.C.
Cohen, M.J., Rickles, W.H., & McArthur, D.L. (1978). Evidence for physiological response stereotypy in migraine headache. *Psychosomatic Medicine*, 40, 344-354.
Corson, J.A. (1964). The effect of human presence on the extinction performance of a cat. *Psychonomic Science*, 1, 413-414.
Corson, J.A. (1976). Families as mutual control systems: Optimization by systematization of reinforcement. In E.J. Mash, L.A. Hamerlynck, L.C. Handy, (Eds.), *Behavior modification and families*. (pp. 317-330). New York: Brunner/Mazel.
Corson, J.A., Bouchard, C., Scherer, M.W., et al. (1973). Instrumental control of

autonomic responses with the use of a cognitive strategy. *Canadian Psychiatric Association Journal*, 18, 21-24.

Corson, J.A., Schneider, M.J., Biondi C.G., & Myers, H.K. (1980). Psychophysiological assessment: Toward a general strategy. *American Journal of Clinical Biofeedback*, 3, 52-67.

Corson, J.A. & Schneider, M.J. (1984). The Dartmouth Pain Questionnaire. *Pain,*19, 59-69.

Deffenbacher, J.L., Demm, P.M. & Brandon, A. D. (1986). High general anger: Correlates and treatment. *Behavior Research & Therapy*, 24 (4), 481-489.

Denicola, J. & Sandler, J. (1980). Training abusive parents in child management and self-control skills. *Behavior Therapy, II*, 263-270.

Drabman, R.S. & Jarvie, G. (1977). Counseling parents of children with behavior problems: The use of extinction and time-out techniques. *Pediatrics*, 59, 78-85.

Elliott, F.A. (1982). Neurological findings in adult minimal brain dysfunction and the dyscontrol syndrome. *Journal of Nervous and Mental Disease*, 170, 680-687.

Ekman, P., Levenson, R.W., Friesen, W.V. (1983). Autonomic nervous system activity distinguishes among emotions. *Science*, 221, 1208- 1210.

Engel, G. L. (1980). The clinical application of the biopsychosocial model. *American Journal of Psychiatry*, 137 (5), 535-544.

Epstein, S. (1973). The self-concept revisited, or a theory of a theory. *American Psychologist*, 28, 404-416.

Epstein, S. (1980). The self-concept: A review and the proposal of an integrated theory of personality. In E. Staub (Ed.), *Personality: Basic aspects and current research*. Englewood Cliffs, NJ: Prentice-Hall.

Epstein, N. (1980). Social consequences of assertion, aggression, passive aggression, and submission: Situational and dispositional determinants. *Behavior Therapy* , ll, 662-669.

Eron, L.D. (1987). The development of aggressive behavior from the perspective of a developing behaviorism. *American Psychologist*, 42 (5), 435-442.

Everly, G. & Sobelman, S.A. (1987). *Assessment of the human stress response.* New York: AMS Press.

Fahrenberg, J., Foerster, F., Schneider, H.J., Muller, W. & Myrtek, M. (1986). Predictability of individual differences in activation processes in a field setting based on laboratory measures. *Psychophysiology*, 23 (3), 323-332.

Feallock, R. & Miller, L.K. (1976). The design and evaluation of a worksharing system for experimental group living. Journal of Applied Behavior Analysis, 9, 277-288.

Feldman, R.G., & Paul, N.L. (1976). Identity of emotional triggers in epilepsy. *Journal of Nervous and Mental Disease*, 162 (5), 345-353.

Ferguson, G.A. (1959). *Statistical analysis in psychology and education.* New York: McGraw Hill.

Feshbach, S. (1970). Aggression. In P.H. Mussen (Ed.), *Carmichael's manual of child psychology* (Vol. 2). New York: Wiley.

Fitzgerald, H.E. & Brackbill, Y. (1976). Classical conditioning in infancy:

Development and constraints. *Psychological Bulletin*, 83, 353-376.

Flor, H., Turk, D.C., & Birbaumer, N. (1985). Assessment of stress-related psychophysiological reactions in chronic back pain patients. *Journal of Consulting and Clinical Psychology*, 53, 354-364.

Fowles, D.C. (1980). The three arousal model: Implications of Gray's two-factor learning theory for heart rate, electrodermal activity, and psychopathy. *Psychophysiology*, 17 (2), 87-103.

Foy, D.W., Eisler, R.M. & Pinkston, S. (1975). Modeled assertion in a case of explosive rage. *Journal of Behavior Therapy and Experimental Psychiatry*, 6, 135-137.

Freud, S. (1930). *Civilization and its discontents.* Standard Edition, London: Hogarth Press, 21, 59. [as cited by Gaylin (1984)].

Frodi, A.M., & Lamb, M.E. (1980). Child abusers' responses to infant smiles and cries. *Child Development*, 51, 238-241.

Garbutt, J.C. & Loosen, P.T. (1983). Is carbamazepine helpful in paroxysmal behavior disorders? *American Journal of Psychiatry*, 140 (10), 1363-1364.

Gaylin, W. (1984). *The rage within.* New York: Simon and Schuster.

Gendreau, P. & Ross, R.R. (1987). Revivification of rehabilitation: Evidence from the 1980's. *Justice Quarterly*, 4 (3), 349-407.

Goldfried, M., Decenteceo, E., & Weinberg, L. (1974). Systematic rational restructuring as a self-control technique. *Behavior Therapy*, 5, 247-254.

Goleman, D. (1985). *Vital lies, simple truths.* New York: Simon & Schuster.

Goodwin, S.E., & Mahoney, M.J. (1975). Modification of aggression through modeling: An experimental probe. *Journal of Behavior Therapy & Experimental Psychiatry*, 6, 200-202.

Greendyke, R.M., Kanter, D.R., Schuster, D.B., Verstreate, S. & Wootton, J. (1986). Propranolol treatment of assaultive patients with organic brain disease. A double–blind crossover, placebo–controlled study. *The Journal of Nervous and Mental Disease*, 174 (5), 290-294.

Harris, T.A. (1967). *I'm OK--You're OK. A practical guide to transactional analysis.* New York: Harper & Row.

Harvey, J.R., Karan, O.C., Bhargava, D. & Morehouse, N. (1978). Relaxation training and cognitive behavioral procedures to reduce violent temper outbursts in a moderately retarded woman. *Journal of Behavior Therapy & Experimental Psychiatry*, 9, 347-351.

Hatch, J.P., Fisher, J.G. & Rugh, J.D. (1987). *Biofeedback: Studies in clinical efficacy.* NY: Plenum.

Hays, J.R., Roberts, T.K., & Solway, K.S. (Eds.). (1981). *Violence and the violent individual.* New York: Spectrum.

Hazaleus, S. L., & Deffenbacher, J.L. (1986). Relaxation and cognitive treatments of anger. *Journal of Consulting and Clinical Psychology*, 54, 222-226.

Heath, L., Kruttschnitt, C., & Ward, D. (1986). Television and violent criminal behavior: Beyond the bobo doll. *Violence and Victims*, 1 (3), 177-190.

Hebb, D.O. (1949). *Organization of behavior.* New York: Wiley.

Hebb, D.O. (1960). The American revolution. *American Psychologist*, 15, 735-745.

Hebb, D.O. (1980). *Essay on Mind*. Hillsdale, New Jersey: Laurence Erlbaum Associates.

Hebb, D.O. (1972). *Textbook of psychology*. Philadelphia, PA: W.B. Saunders Co.

Holmes, T.H., & Rahe, R.H. (1967). The social readjustment rating scale. *Journal of Psychosomatic Research*, 11, 213-218.

Holden, C. (1987). The genetics of personality. *Science*, 237, 598-601.

Horowitz, M.J. (1981). Self-righteous rage and the attribution of blame. *Archives of General Psychiatry*, 38, 1233-1238.

Houtler, B.D. & Rosenberg, H. (1985). The retrospective baseline in single case experiments. *The Behavior Therapist*, 8, 97-98.

Hughes, J.R. & Hermann, B.P. (1984). Evidence of psychopathology in patients with rhythmic midtemporal discharges. *Biological Psychiatry*, 19, 1623-1634.

Hunt, J.McV. (1972). Early childhood education and social class. *Canadian Psychologist*, 13, 305-328.

Infantino, J.A., Jr. & Musingo, S.Y. (1985). Assaults and injuries among staff with and without training in aggression control techniques. *Hospital and Community Psychiatry*, 36 (12), 1312-1314.

Itil, T.M. & Wadud, A. (1975). Treatment of human aggression with major tranquilizers, antidepressants and newer psychotropic drugs. *The Journal of Nervous and Mental Disease*, 160 (2), 83-99.

James, W. (1892). *Psychology: Briefer course*. New York: Holt.

James, W. (1907). *Pragmatism: A new name for some old ways of thinking*. New York: Longmans, Green.

Kazdin, A.E. & Bootzin, R.R. (1972). The token economy: An evaluative review. *Journal of Applied Behavior Analysis*, 5, 343-372.

Keller, S. (1963). The social world of the urban slum child: Some early findings. *American Journal of Orthopsychiatry*, 33, 823-831.

Kelly, G.A. (1955). The psychology of personal constructs. New York: Norton.

Kinkade, K. (1973). *A Walden-Two experiment: The first five years of twin oaks community*. New York: William Morrow.

Kolata, G. (1987). What babies know and noises parents make. *Science*, 237, 726.

Kolb, L.C. (1987). A neuropsychological hypothesis explaining posttraumatic stress disorders. *American Journal of Psychiatry*, 144 (8), 989-995.

Lane, R.D. & Schwartz, G.E. (1987). Induction of lateralized sympathetic input to the heart by the CNS during emotional arousal: A possible neurophysiologic trigger of sudden cardiac death. *Psychosomatic Medicine*, 49 (3), 274-284.

Lang, P.J. (1979). A bio-informational theory of emotional imagery. *Psychophysiology*, 16 (6), 495-512.

Levine, L., Garcia Coll, C.T. & Oh, W. (1985). Determinants of mother-infant interaction in adolescent mothers. *Pediatrics*, 75 (1), 23-29.

Lewinsohn, P.M., Weinstein, M.S., & Shaw, D.A. (1968). Depression: A clinical-research approach. In R.D. Rubin & C.M. Franks (Eds.). *Advances in Behavior Therapy*. New York: Academic Press.

Lion, J.R., Madden, D.J. & Christopher, R.L. (1976). A violence clinic: Three years' experience. *American Journal of Psychiatry*, 133 (4), 432-435.

Long, B.H. & Henderson, E.H. (1967). Social schemata of school beginners: Some demographic correlates. *Proceedings of the 75th Annual Convention of the American Psychological Association*, Washington, D.C.: American Psychological Association, 329-330.

Lorr, M. & Wunderlich, R.A. (1986). Two objective measures of self-esteem. *Journal of Personality Assessment*, 50 (1), 18-23

Luiselli, J.K. (1984). Treatment of an assaultive, sensory-impaired adolescent through a multicomponent behavioral program. *Journal of Behavior Therapy and Experimental Psychiatry*, 15 (1), 71-78.

MacLean, P.D. (1986). Ictal symptoms relating to the nature of affects and their cerebral substrate. In R. Plutchik, & H. Kellerman, (Eds.), *Biological foundations of emotion* (pp. 61-90). New York: Academic Press.

Maitland, S.C. (1966). *The perspective, frustration-failure and delay of gratification in middle-class and lower-class children from organized and disorganized families*. Unpublished doctoral dissertation, University of Minnesota, Minneapolis.

Mandelzys, N., Lane, E.B. & Marceau, R. (1981). The relationship of violence to alpha levels in a biofeedback training paradigm. *Journal of Clinical Psychology*, 37 (1), 202-209.

Markus, H. & Nurius, P. (1986). Possible selves: *American Psychologist*, 41 (9), 954-969.

Markus, H. & Nurius, P. (1986). Possible selves: The interface between motivation and the self-concept. In K. Yardley & T. Honess, (Eds.). *Self and identity: Psychosocial perspectives* (pp. 157-172). New York: Wiley.

Masters, J.C., Burish, T.G., Hollon, S.D. & Rimm, D.C. (1987). *Behavior therapy: Techniques and empirical findings*. (3rd ed.). New York: Harcourt, Brace, Jovanovich.

Megargee, E.I. (1966). Undercontrolled and overcontrolled personality types in extreme antisocial aggression. *Psychological Monographs*, 3, (Whole No. 611).

Meichenbaum, D. (1974). *Cognitive behavior modification*. Morristown, NJ.: General Learning Press.

Meichenbaum, D. (1977). *Cognitive behavior modification: An integrative approach*. New York: Plenum Press.

Meichenbaum, D. (1980). Stability of Personality: Change and psychotherapy. In E. Staub (Ed.), *Personality: Basic aspects and current research*. Englewood Cliffs, NJ: Prentice-Hall.

Miller, A. (1984). *For your own good*. New York: Farrar, Straus & Giroux (Second Edition).

Miller, W.R. & Seligman, M.E.P. (1976). Learned helplessness, depression and the perception of reinforcement. *Behavior Research and Therapy*, 14, 7-17.

Mischel, W. (1976). *Introduction to personality* (2nd ed.). New York: Holt, Rinehart and Winston.

Mischel, W. & Metzner, R. (1962). Preference for delayed reward as a function of age, intelligence and length of delay interval. *Journal of Abnormal and Social*

Psychology, 64, 245-431.

Monroe, R.R. (1975). Anticonvulsants in the treatment of aggression. *The Journal of Nervous and Mental Disease*, 160 (2), 119-126

Moos, R. (1973). Conceptualizations of human environments. *American Psychologist*, 28, 652-665.

Moos, R. (1976). *The human context: Environmental determinants of behavior.* New York: Wiley.

Moos, R.H. (1969). Sources of variance in responses to questionnaires and in behavior. *Journal of Abnormal Psychology*, 74, 405-412.

Moos, R.H. & Insel, P.M. (Eds.). (1974). *Issues in social ecology.* Palo Alto, CA: National Press Books.

Murray, H.A. (with collaborators) (1938). *Explorations in personality.* New York: Oxford University Press.

Newmark, C.S. (Ed.). (1985). *Major psychological assessment instruments.* Boston: Allyn & Bacon.

Novaco, R.W. (1975). *Anger control: The development and evaluation of an experimental treatment.* Lexington, MA: Heath.

Novaco, R.W. (1976). The functions and regulation of the arousal of anger. *American Journal of Psychiatry*, 133,1124-1128.

Peterson, C. & Seligman, M.E.P. (1984). Causal explanations as a risk factor for depression: Theory and evidence. *Psychological Review*, 91, 347-374.

Rachman, S. & Lopatka, C. (1986). Match and mismatch in the prediction of fear - I. *Behavior Research & Therapy*, 24, (3), 387-393.

Rachman, S. & Loptaka, C. (1986). Match and mismatch of fear in Gray's theory - II. *Behavior Research & Therapy*, 24, (4), 395-401.

Ratey, J.J., Morrill, R., & Oxenkrug, G. (1983). Use of propranolol for provoked and unprovoked episodes of rage. *American Journal of Psychiatry*, 140 (10), 1356-1357.

Rehm, L.P. & Plakosh, P. (1975). Preference for immediate reinforcement in depression. *Journal of Behavior Therapy & Experimental Psychiatry*, 6, 101-103.

Riley, T. & Niedermeyer, E. (1977). Rage attacks and episodic violent behavior: Electroencephalographic findings and general considerations. *Clinical Electroencephalography*, 9, 131-139.

Rimm, D.C., de Groot, J.C., Board, P., Heiman, J. & Dillow, P.V. (1971). Systematic desensitization of an anger response. *Behavior Research & Therapy*, 9, 273-280.

Rimm, D.C., & Masters, J.C. (1979). *Behavior therapy: Techniques and empirical findings* (2nd ed.). New York: Academic Press.

Roth, L.H. (Ed.). (1987). *Clinical treatment of the violent person.* New York: Guilford.

Roy, A. (1977). Hysterical fits previously diagnosed as epilepsy. *Psychological Medicine*, 7, 271-273.

Rychlak, J.F. (1977). *The psychology of rigorous humanism.* New York: Wiley.

Samenow, S.E. (1984). *Inside the criminal mind.* New York: Times Books.

Sandler, J., Van Dercar, C., & Milhoan, M. (1978). Training child abusers in the use of positive reinforcement practices. *Behavior Research & Therapy,* 16,169-175.

Sanders, W. (1978). Systematic densensitization in the treatment of child abuse. *American Journal of Psychiatry,* 135, 483-484.

Schatzman, M. (1973). *Soul murder: Persecution in the family.* New York: Penguin.

Seligman, M.E.P. (1975). *Helplessness: On depression, development and death.* San Francisco: W.H. Freeman.

Selye, H. (1974). *Stress without distress.* Philadelphia: Lippincott.

Selye, H. (1976). *The stress of life.* New York: McGraw-Hill.

Selye, H. (1978, March). On the real benefits of eustress. *Psychology Today,* 60-64.

Skinner, B.F. (1948). *Walden two.* New York: Macmillan.

Skinner, B.F. (1961, Summer). The design of cultures. *Daedalus,* pp. 534-546.

Skinner, B.F. (1971). *Beyond freedom and dignity.* New York: Knopf.

Smith, J.S. (1980). Episodic rage. In M. Girgis & L.G. Kiloh (Eds.), *Limbic epilepsy and the dyscontrol syndrome.* Amsterdam: Elsvier.

Staub, E. (Ed.). (1980). *Personality: Basic aspects and current research.* Englewood Cliffs, NJ: Prentice-Hall.

Steen, M.T. (1966). *The effects of immediate and delayed reinforcement on the achievement behavior of Mexican- American children of low socio-economic status.* Unpublished doctoral dissertation, Stanford University, California.

Stone, J.L., McDaniel, K.D., Hughes, J.R. & Hermann, B.P. (1986). Episodic dyscontrol disorder and paroxysmal EEG abnormalities: Successful treatment with carbamazepine. *Biological Psychiatry,* 21, 208-212.

Stringer, A.Y. & Josef, N.C. (1983). Methylphenidate in the treatment of aggression in two patients with antisocial personality disorder. *American Journal of Psychiatry,* 140 (10), 1365-1366.

Stroebel, C. (1982). *QR the quieting reflex.* New York: Berkley Books.

Sweetland, R.C. & Keyser, D.J. (1983). *Tests.* Kansas City: Test Corporation of America.

Tardiff, K. (1987). Violence and the violent patient. In R.E. Hales & A.J. Frances (Eds.), *Psychiatry update: The American Psychiatric Association Annual Review,* 6, 447–566.

Terrel, G., Jr., Durkin, K. & Weisley, M. (1959). Social class and the nature of the incentive in discrimination learning. Journal of *Abnormal & Social Psychology,* 59, 270-272.

Tharp, R.G. & Gallimore, R. (1976). Basketball's John Wooden: What a coach can teach a teacher. *Psychology Today,* 9, 74-78.

Van der Kolk, B.A. & Greenberg, M.S. (1987). The psychobiology of the trauma response: Hyperarousal, constriction, and addiction to traumatic reexposure. In B.A. Van der Kolk (Ed.), *Psychological Trauma* (pp. 63-87). Washington, D.C.: American Psychiatric Press.

Wallace, J. (1966). An abilities conception of personality: Some implications for personality measurement. *American Psychologist,* 21, 132-138.

Wallin B.G. & Fagius, J. (1986, February). The sympathetic nervous system in man

- aspects derived from microelectrode recordings. *Trends in Neuroscience*, pp. 63-73.

Weilburg, J.B., Bear, D.M. & Sachs, G. (1987). Three patients with concomitant panic attacks and seizure disorder: Possible clues to the neurology of anxiety. *American Journal of Psychiatry*, 144 (8), 1053-1056.

White, M.A. (1975). Natural rates of teacher approval and disapproval in the classroom. *Journal of Applied Behavior Analysis*, 8, 367-372.

Willerman, L., Turner, R.G. & Peterson, M.A. (1976). A comparison of the predictive validity of typical and maximal personality measures. *Journal of Research in Personality*, 10, 482-492.

Wong, S.E., Slama, K.M. & Liberman, R.P. (1987). Behavioral analysis and therapy for aggressive psychiatric and developmentally disabled patients. In L.H. Roth (Ed.). *Clinical treatment of the violent person.* New York: Guilford.

Yudofsky, S.C., Silver, J.M., Jackson, W., Endicott, J. & Williams, D. (1986). The overt aggression scale for the objective rating of verbal and physical aggression. *American Journal of Psychiatry*, 143 (1), 35-39.

Zigler, E. & deLabry, J. (1962). Concept-switching in middle-class, lower-class and retarded children. *Journal of Abnormal and Social Psychology*, 65, 267-273.

INDEX

ABC chart/diagram, 4, 92–95, 104
Abuse, 37, 66–70, 71–82, 216–219
Abusive parents, 66–82
Adler, A., xii, 126
Almy, T., 12, 13, 143
Allport, G., 12
Alpha press, 14
Anger, 142–158, 208, 220, 225
ANS (see autonomic)
Ansbacher, H., xii
Assessment, 8–9, 91–93, 136–159, 206–207, 223–224
Autonomic nervous system, 26–33, 107, 119, 136–159, 225

Bandura, A., 42, 44
Binary switch, 19, 20, 23
Bindra, D., xii, 28, 39, 42
Biofeedback, 3, 107–116, 136–159, 225
Biological variables, xiii, 25–33
Biopsychosocial, 2, 3, 5, 18, 131, 136, 223
Bulimia, 92, 94, 99–104

Cattell, R.B., 12, 14
Central motive state, 27–33, 191, 224

Children (see also preverbal), 37–87
Christopherson, E.R., 72
Cleghorn, A., 107
Cleghorn, R.A., xiii, 107
Cognitive, 11, 107
Cognitive behavior therapy, 136, 143
Cognitive structures, 25
Co–investigator (client as co–investigator), 97, 105, 223–224
Compelling situations, 14, 15, 224
Contracts, 39–54, 56–70, 73
Critic function, 18, 71, 127–129
Critical audience (see also essential audience), 18, 127
Critics, heros and monsters, 127–129

Dartmouth Pain Questionnaire, 91, 109
Definitions and postulates, 5–12, 14–24, 26–33
Disposition, 5, 18, 159, 191, 195, 224, 227

Early environment, 42–47, 119
Electrodermal (see also skin conductance), 113, 137

EEG, 119, 136, 173–174, 182,
194, 211
EMG, 27, 109–110
Emotion (see also emotional fire
in the boiler and autonomic),11,
26–33
Emotional fire in the boiler (see
also autonomic), 26–33, 129,
131, 191, 195, 224, 228
Environment, 11
Episodic dyscontrol, 118, 130,
136, 173–174
Epstein, S., 9, 41
Erg, 14
Essential audience (see also
critic; critic function), 18, 33,
37, 84, 191
Eustress, 6
Evaluation, 112–116
Exhibitionists, 92, 95
Expectancies, xi, 5, 18, 26, 159,
191, 195, 224, 227
Expectations, xi, 176

Failure signals, xi
Families, 37–87
Feared possible selves, 16–33,
191, 216–219
Ferguson, G., xiii
Fire in the boiler (see also autonomic
and emotional), 26–33, 129, 131,
191, 195, 224, 228
Flow diagram, 97–106
Follow–up, 145–159
Freud, S., 12, 132, 228

Goleman, D., 86, 87
Greenberg, M.S., (see Van der
Kolk, B.A.)
Habituation, 158–159
Hebb, D.O., xii, xiii, 17, 21
Heart rate, 26

Heroes (see critics)
Homeostasis, 42, 43
Hoped for possible selves, 16–33, 191
Horowitz, M., 125–129
Hostility, 145–159
Hyperarousal and the binary
switch, 87, 119–121

Ideographic (see individual
differences), 1
Incentive stimuli inverted, 84–87
Incentive theory, 39, 42, 84–86
Individual differences, xii–xiv,
158–159
Internal dialogue, 20–23, 26, 176, 191,
195

James, W., 21

Kelly, G., 8, 19, 21

Learning, xii, 39
Level setting (see also autonomic and
priming), 26–33, 121–124, 174
Looking for trouble, 124–126, 174

Markus, H., 16, 17
Meichenbaum, D., 20–22, 25, 136
Memory, xii
Method, 55–70, 107–116, 136–159
Microanalysis, 11, 13
Miller, A., 37, 38, 60, 70, 216
Milsum, J., 2
Minimodels, 3, 13, 91–95, 144, 196
Mischel, W., 9
Models, 144, 196
Modeling, 1, 3, 13, 91–95, 144, 196
Monsters (see critics)
Motive (see central motive state)
Multilevel model, 3–4, 13, 91–95,
144, 196
Murray, H.A., 14

Mutual control systems, 37–54

Negative reinforcement, 18–19, 40,
  196, 216–219
Neurological correlates, 118–119, 136
Nomothetic, xiii, 1
Novaco, R.W., 21
Nurius, P., 16–17

Pain, 109–113
Parasympathetic (see autonomic), 26
Parental attention, 18, 37–87, 216–219
Personal Scientist/Personal Theorist,
  19–20, 22, 97, 177, 223–224, 227
Personality, 7, 11, 14, 144, 223,
  227–228
Personality and society, 227–228
Personality theory, 11–24, 144,
  223
Physical punishment, 37, 60–70
Physiological data, 146–159
Physiological monitoring (see also
  biofeedback), 3, 137–159
Placebo, 158–159
PNS (see parasympathetic)
Point of view, 22, 29
Population, 133
Positive expectancies, xi
Possible selves, 16–33, 176, 191, 216
Post traumatic stress, 124–125, 183
Preverbal children, 71–82
Priming, 5, 121–124, 130–131, 174
Profiling, 7, 115–116, 118, 137–159
Psychophysiological profile, 7,
  137–159
Punishment, 37

Quick calming response (see
  relaxation), 207–208, 211

Recommended reading, 131–132
Record keeping, 137–142, 144–159

Reinforcement, 39–54, 216–219
Reinforcement schedules, 40, 85
Relaxation, 31, 136, 142–144,
  207–208, 211
Results, 62–70, 144–159
Role playing, 3, 143, 208, 228
Rychlak, J., 21

Sample, 13, 133–136
Schatzman, M., 86
Secondary gains, 126
Seizures, 130, 173–174
Self concept, xi, 1, 5, 7, 12, 14,
  17, 19, 41–54, 91, 124, 129–130,
  215–219
Self esteem, 54, 69, 85, 215–216
Self satisfaction, 91–93, 139, 184, 224
Self–schema, 17–18
Seligman, M.E. P., 15, 86
Selye, H., xiv, 5–6
Sense of agency, 41, 54, 69, 227
Shifting biases, 12
Shifty defined, 12
Shifty theory of personality, 9, 11–24,
  91–93, 223
Shifting variables, 19, 223
Skill acquisition, 158–159, 196
Skin conductance, 26–27, 119,
  146–159, 169, 175–177, 185, 207
Skin resistance (see skin conductance)
Skinner, B.F., 38–40, 69–70
Slamecka, N.J., xii
SNS (see sympathetic)
Society (see personality and society)
Spasms, 109–113
Stimulus value, 5, 125
Stress, xi, xiv, 5, 14
Stress and individual differences, 14
Stress innoculation, 136
Stress interview, 143–159, 169,195
Stress profiling, 7, 115–116, 118,
  137–159, 169, 177, 185

Sympathetic nervous system (see also
    autonomic and emotional and skin
    conductance), 26–33, 119,
    130–131
Systematic desensitization, 136
Systematic parental attention, 58–60
Systems theory, 1, 5–9, 30
Systems dynamics modeling, 2, 30

Therapeutic possibilities, 128–131
Threats, 219–221
Time–out, 78–82
Treatment adaptations, 206–214
Treatment methods, 136–159,
    223–224

Van der Kolk, B.A., 120–124
Violent behavior, 5, 13, 20, 27,
    117–228
Violent clients as examples for
    theorizing, 13

Wallace, J., 15
Working self concept (see possible
    selves), 176, 191,195, 216, 221,
    223–224